ART
FOR CHILDREN

A STEP-BY-STEP GUIDE FOR
THE YOUNG ARTIST

Danielle
   from
      Grammy
Use your talent!

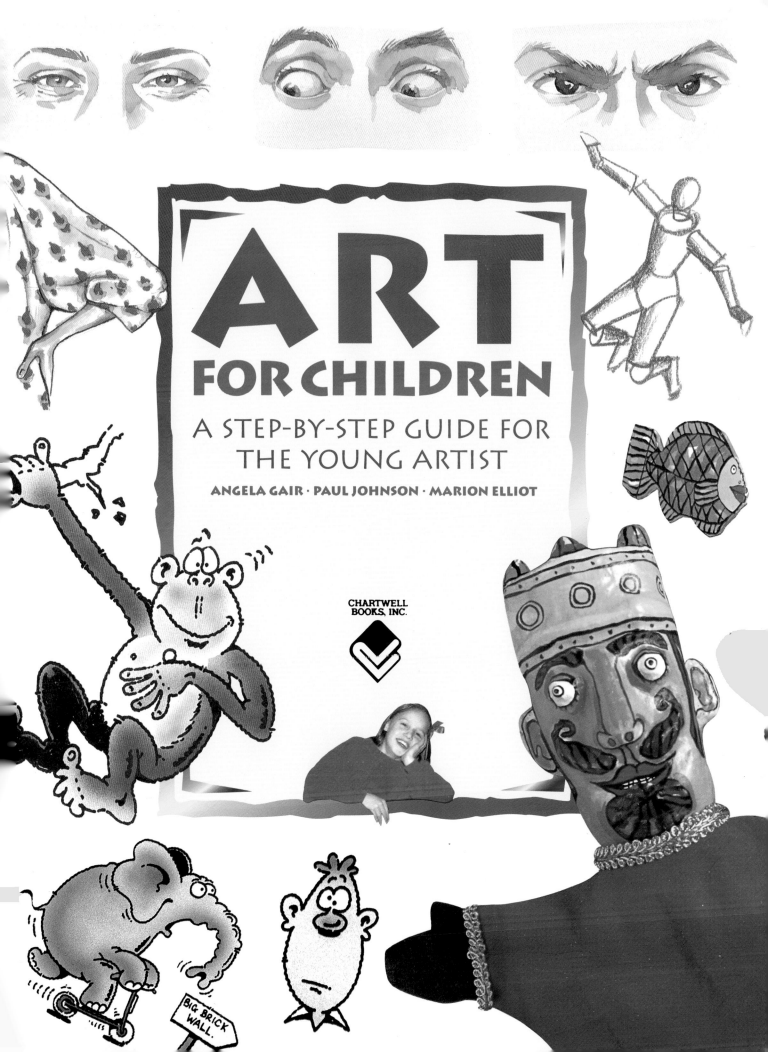

ART
FOR CHILDREN

A STEP-BY-STEP GUIDE FOR
THE YOUNG ARTIST

ANGELA GAIR · PAUL JOHNSON · MARION ELLIOT

CHARTWELL
BOOKS, INC.

BIG BRICK WALL.

A QUARTO BOOK

ISBN: 0–7858–0517–6

This book was designed and produced by
Quarto Children's Books Limited
The Fitzpatrick Building
188–194 York Way
London N7 9QP

Manufactured in Hong Kong by
Regent Publishing Services Limited.

Published by Chartwell Books
A Division of Book Sales, Inc.
114 Northfield Avenue
Edison, New Jersey 08837

Reprinted in 1997

CONTENTS

How to Draw and Paint People

How to Draw and Paint Cartoons

Papier Mache Project Book

Getting started

Anyone can paint and draw people – it is just a matter of developing the talent. It is like learning to play football, or tennis, or a musical instrument – practice every day and you will find you get better and better. This book will give you lots of ideas to try out at home or at school.

There are all sorts of different paints, papers and drawing materials in the shops. It is important to choose the right materials for each kind of artwork. They are described in later chapters – but here are some items you will need when you start painting and drawing.

Brushes

It is important to have good paint brushes. The ones that come in most painting sets aren't very good – they are too floppy and the hairs fall out. Ask for brushes made of hog's hair or nylon. They are not too expensive, and they last a long time. You will need a small watercolor brush that comes to a point, for painting small details, and a large brush with a longer handle for painting big shapes.

Paper

There are several kinds of paper, and it comes in a variety of colors. You can buy paper in sheets or in pads. *Newsprint* is fine if you are using powder paints, pastels or crayons. An *all-purpose paper* has a nice surface for pencil drawing. You can buy special paper for painting in watercolor. Because it is white, it makes your paint colors really sparkle. It is also a good idea to buy a small sketch pad which you can carry around with you.

Paint palettes

You can buy special paint palettes for mixing your paints, but old dishes and plates do just as well – the bigger the better, so you have plenty of room to mix your colors.

Drawing board

You will need a hard surface to support your paper when you draw and paint. You can buy one ready-made, or make one from blockboard or plywood. Use clips or thumbtacks to attach the paper to the board.

Tips

So you've bought your paint, papers and brushes and you're ready to paint a masterpiece! Here are some tips to help you get started.

● **Keep it clean** Wear old clothes when you are painting, or borrow an old shirt to protect your clothes from paint splashes.

● **Get organized** Make sure you have everything you need *before* you start.

● **Prevent accidents** Give yourself lots of room; it will stop you spilling water jars or knocking things onto the floor. If you are right-handed keep your paints and water jar on your right side, or the other way round if you are left-handed. This stops you dripping paint on your paper when you reach over to dip your brush.

● **Save it** Save money, and help protect the environment by re-using materials that normally get thrown away. For instance, save old jars, dinner plates and plastic pots for mixing paints. (Liquid detergent bottles with the tops cut off are useful too.) Cut up old clothes to make rags for mopping up. Collect newspapers for protecting your work table (and the floor!) Save small objects like bottle tops, buttons, dried pasta shapes and shiny sweet wrappers for when you make collage pictures. Use scrap paper for testing pencils, brushes and paint mixes.

Drawing heads

Before you learn how to draw the different features of the face – the eyes, ears, nose and mouth – you first need to know how to draw heads, and how to find the correct position to place the features on the face. It is difficult to know where to begin. Sometimes we make the nose too long, or place the eyes too high up on the face. Sometimes we put the mouth too low, or the ears in the wrong place. Here are some tips that will help you avoid making mistakes.

How the head sits on the neck
When you draw a figure, be careful not to draw the neck too thin. The drawing on the right is correct. The neck is nearly as wide as the face (check this for yourself by looking in the mirror!)

Arty says...
Cut out faces and heads from magazines and newspapers and trace over them. It's a good way to learn where the features are positioned.

How to draw a head
Seen from the front, the head is shaped like an egg, with the pointed end down.

Start by drawing the shape of the head. Then draw a line down the middle of the head. This gives you the position for the nose and the centre of the mouth.

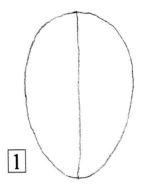

1

The hairline is about one-third down from the top of the head to the eyes.

Draw a line across the middle of the head. This is where the eyes are positioned.

2

The eyes are halfway down the head.

The ears line up between the eyebrows and the tip of the nose.

The tip of the nose is halfway between the eyebrows and the bottom of the chin.

The lower lip is halfway between the tip of the nose and the bottom of the chin.

Draw another line halfway below that. This is where the tip of the nose will come. Draw another line halfway between the nose line and the bottom of the chin. This is where the mouth will go. Now you can draw in the eyes, nose and mouth in their correct positions. The ears line up between the eyebrows and the tip of the nose.

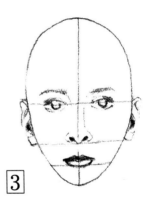

3

Egg-heads

We don't always see people's faces from straight in front. When someone is looking up, down, or to one side, their head is tilted at an angle – and this makes the features even more difficult to draw! You can make a simple model that will help you to see what happens to the features of the face when the head is tilted at different angles.

Make drawings of your egg-head model from different angles.

Take a hard-boiled egg and hold it pointed end down. Using the measuring method above, draw eyes and a mouth on the egg. Make a nose out of plasticine and stick it on the egg. Tip the "egg-head" forwards, backwards and to either side.

Eyes

When we look at a person, we usually notice their eyes first. The eyes are the most expressive feature of the face – they can tell us a lot about a person's feelings.

Eyes differ in shape, size and color from one person to another. But everyone's eyes are made in the same way. You will find it easier to draw and paint eyes if you understand how they are formed. Let's take a closer look at eyes.

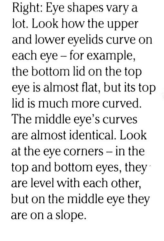

Below: It helps to understand how eyes fit into the skull in order to draw them. You only see part of an eyeball – the rest is hidden behind the eyelids. Use your fingertip gently to feel the roundness of your eyeballs through your upper eyelids.

With what you know about eye shapes, you can start drawing them in step-by-step stages.

Right: Eye shapes vary a lot. Look how the upper and lower eyelids curve on each eye – for example, the bottom lid on the top eye is almost flat, but its top lid is much more curved. The middle eye's curves are almost identical. Look at the eye corners – in the top and bottom eyes, they are level with each other, but on the middle eye they are on a slope.

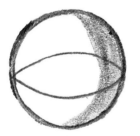

1 To draw an eye from the front, draw a circle for the eyeball. Add eyelids, with the corners on the ball sides.

2 Outline the pupil, and add a line to show the eyelid thickness. Shade the dark side of the eyeball.

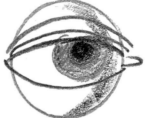

3 Color the iris; add a small loop on the right corner for the tear duct. A rough line shows the eyebrow.

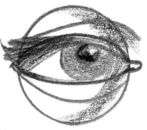

4 Add eyelashes to complete the eye. Highlights on the iris and pupil will make the eye look really round and shiny.

1 The opening of an eye seen from the side looks like a slice of cake, with its corner in the eyeball center.

2 Add shading to one side of your eyeball to give it real shape and a feeling of solidity.

3 When you draw the iris and the pupil, you will not be able to see all of them – they should be oval shaped.

4 Finish the eye with some eyelashes – don't forget that upper eyelashes are longer than lower ones.

The distance between eyes varies slightly from person to person. Usually, however, you'll find the distance between the two inner eye corners is about one eye width, as shown right.

Your eyes are a dead giveaway when it comes to showing your emotions! Without looking at the captions to the pairs of eyes below, see if you can tell what sort of emotion each pair of eyes is showing.

This person's eyes have been crying – the edges of the eyelids are red, and there are shiny highlights on the lower eyelids.

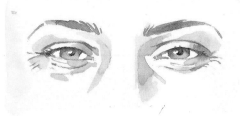

This pair of eyes suggest someone smiling. The eyes look straight forward and there are wrinkles – "laughter lines" – around the eye.

This person looks worried and thoughtful – perhaps he's wondering how he did in an exam!

If you are scared of spiders, this is how you'd look if you saw one on your wrist!

You can't believe what you're hearing, and your eyes are wide open in astonishment!

People who are angry squeeze their eyelids together – the closer they are, the angrier the expression.

This portrait of a woman is by Frans Hals, a Dutch artist of the 17th century. Look at the way he has captured the model's expression. Remember that when you smile, you smile not only with your lips, but also with your whole face.

Cover up the mouth in the painting, and you will see that the woman's eyes are smiling, too. When you go to an art gallery, look carefully for the expressions in people's eyes in different pictures.

Look at the difference between the eyes in these three pictures. Babies have big eyes, old people have wrinkly eyes. When you draw or paint someone, make sure you look at the eyes very carefully; they can make a lot of difference to a picture!

Some common mistakes

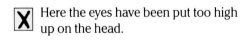 Here the eyes have been put too high up on the head.

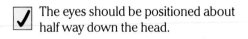 The eyes should be positioned about half way down the head.

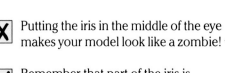 Putting the iris in the middle of the eye makes your model look like a zombie!

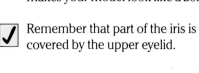 Remember that part of the iris is covered by the upper eyelid.

Mouths

The mouth is a very expressive part of the face. A smiling mouth tells us that someone is happy, but lips that are tight and thin tell us that someone is angry. When you paint or draw a portrait, pay special attention to the mouth, because its shape and expression are part of the character of the face. Here are some useful tips to help you to draw and paint mouths realistically.

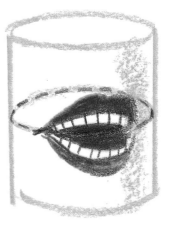

The lips are not flat and straight, but follow the curve of the teeth. Imagine the face as a cylinder – like a can of peas!

When the face is turned a little to one side, you can see the curved shape of the mouth more clearly.

When a person laughs, you can see clearly how the lips are drawn back over the curve of the teeth.

You can show the curved shape of the lips in your paintings and drawings by using the contrast of light and shade. This mouth looks flat because it has been painted all one color.

This mouth looks more realistic because the artist used a darker shade for the shadowed parts of the lips and a lighter shade for the parts that stick out and catch the light.

How to draw the mouth
1 Start by drawing the dark line between the lips.

2 Very lightly draw the outline of the upper and lower lips.

3 Look carefully for the patches of light and shadow on the lips. Start by shading in the lightest parts, using very light pencil strokes.

4 Add more pencil strokes to shade in the dark areas. Don't forget the tiny shadow underneath the bottom lip.

The mouth from the front

Notice how some parts of the lips look paler than others, where the light hits them.

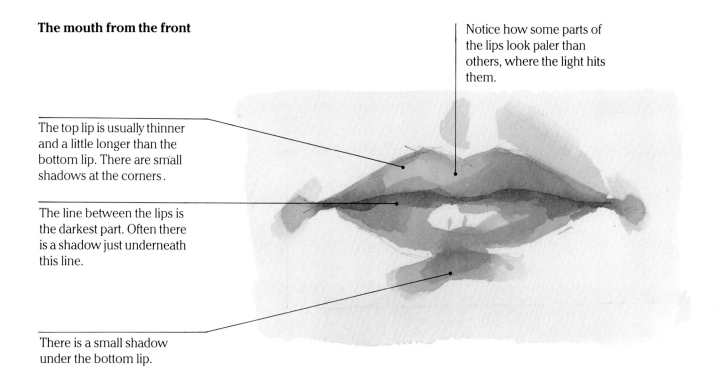

The top lip is usually thinner and a little longer than the bottom lip. There are small shadows at the corners.

The line between the lips is the darkest part. Often there is a shadow just underneath this line.

There is a small shadow under the bottom lip.

The mouth from the side

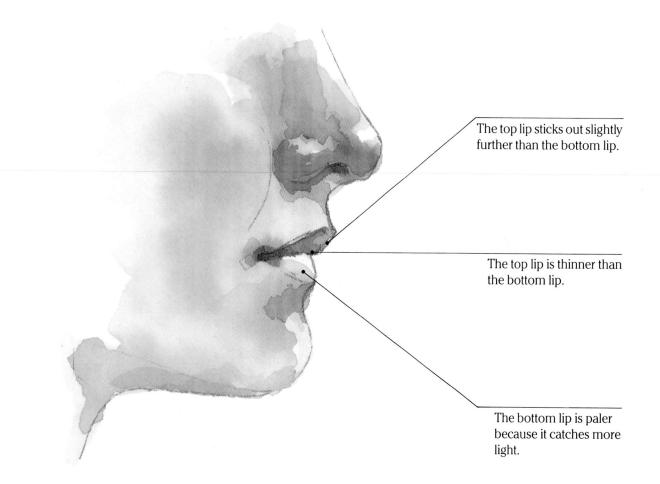

The top lip sticks out slightly further than the bottom lip.

The top lip is thinner than the bottom lip.

The bottom lip is paler because it catches more light.

Babies and small children have small mouths, with plump and full lips.

As people get older, they develop wrinkles around their mouths.

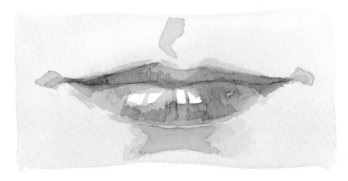

Men's lips are usually longer and narrower than women's lips.

Women tend to have shorter but fuller lips than men's lips.

Laughing lips

Even without the rest of a face, the mouth can tell you what a person is feeling. This picture by the French artist Toulouse-Lautrec, painted in 1899, shows a woman who is obviously happy, enjoying jokes with friends at dinner. More than anything else, her mouth and lips show enjoyment.

The close-up below shows how the artist used bright red paint for the lips, and gave them an exaggerated shape, to draw our attention to them.

There are lots of different ways to draw mouths, though. Compare this picture with the *Mona Lisa* opposite.

You will probably recognize this painting. It is the *Mona Lisa* by Leonardo da Vinci. It is probably the most famous painting in the world. It was painted hundreds of years ago (in 1507). Today it hangs in the Louvre in Paris, and every year thousands of people come to marvel at the mysterious, bewitching smile of the Mona Lisa.

Noses and ears

W hen you draw noses, look carefully at the areas of light and shadow that reveal their form. Leave the light parts white and shade in the shadowed parts. This is how artists show the way the nose sticks out from the face – without light and shadow, the nose would look flat. (Turn to page 48 if you want to learn more about light and shadow.)

Drawing a nose from the front

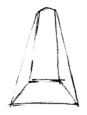  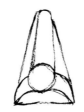

1 The middle section is a wedge shape.

2 The tip is ball-shaped.

3 The nostrils are wing-shaped.

Drawing a nose from the side

  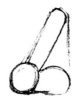

1 The basic shape is a triangle.

2 The tip is ball-shaped.

3 The nostril is wing-shaped.

There is usually a dark shadow beneath the nose, and another shadow down one side. The bridge of the nose (the bony part down the middle) catches the light, and so does the soft tip of the nose. The nostrils are the darkcst parts.

When you have the shape right, rub out the guide lines or draw on top of them and fill in the areas of light and shadow with pencil strokes.

Look at people in a line at the supermarket checkout. You'll see an amazing variety of ears and noses!

Ears

You can draw friends' ears while they watch television or chat. Draw the ears from the front (some people's ears stick out more than others!) Then move around to one side of your model and draw the ear from full view. This is more difficult, because the ear is such a funny shape. When you look into the ear you can see the strange, uncurling forms, as if it was searching for sound. Don't worry if your first drawings are not very good. Keep practicing and you will get better and better!

This drawing shows the position of the ear on the side of the head. It lines up with the eyebrow at the top and the tip of the nose at the bottom. Its position is in the middle of the head – farther away from the face than you might think.

Drawing an ear

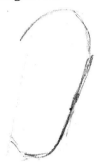

1 Draw the outline of the ear first.

2 Draw the earhole.

3 Fit the spiralling shapes in between.

4 Look for the shadows inside the ear and shade them in.

From the front, the ear is a squashed-up shape. Look for the contrast between light and shadow.

"Identikit" faces

S ee how many different characters you can create by making your own "identikit" set. Trace the outline of one of these faces on a piece of thin white paper. Then choose some eyes, a nose, and a mouth, and trace them onto the face, making sure that you put them in the correct position (as a guide, use the horizontal lines which have been drawn on each face). You can make lots of funny faces by mixing up different features. The features of five different faces are jumbled up here – see if you can match them up correctly.

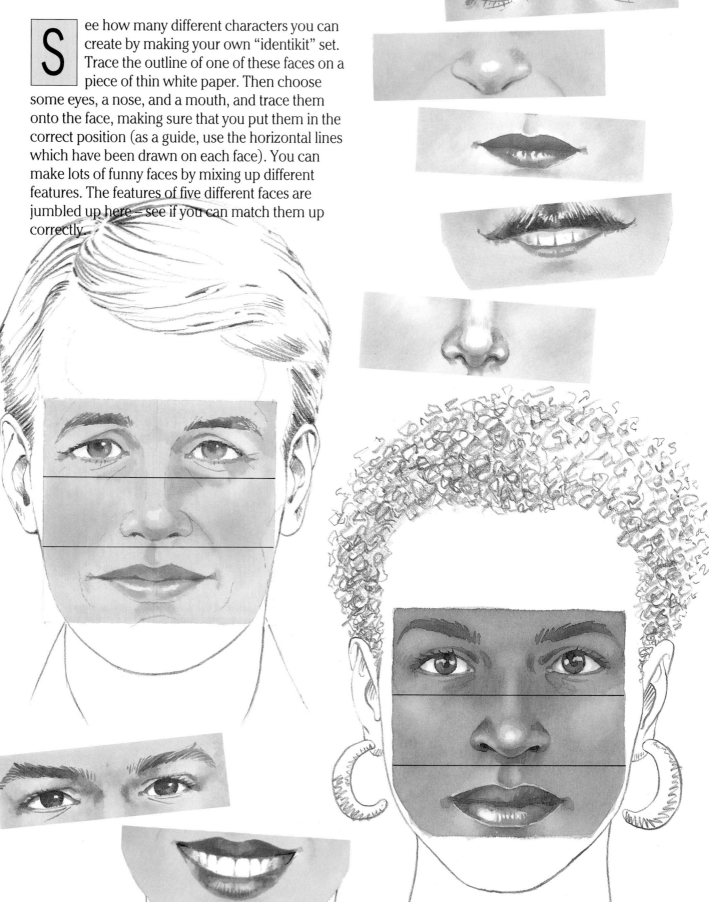

22

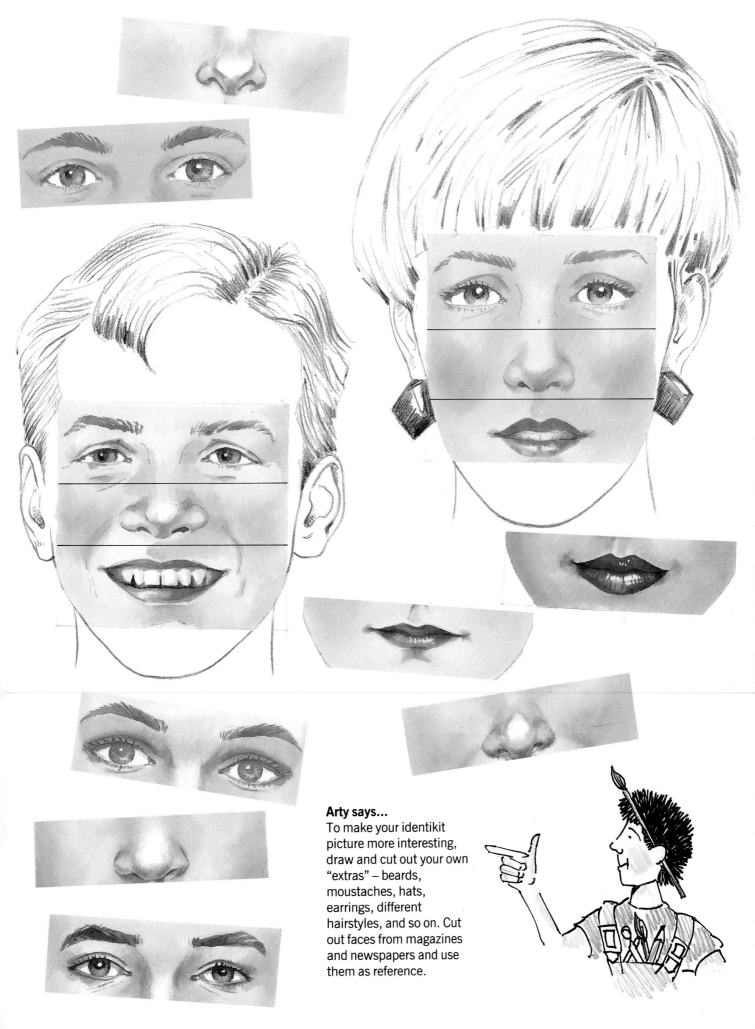

Arty says...
To make your identikit picture more interesting, draw and cut out your own "extras" – beards, moustaches, hats, earrings, different hairstyles, and so on. Cut out faces from magazines and newspapers and use them as reference.

Cartoon time

E veryone loves cartoons. Popeye, Charlie Brown, and Calvin are just some of our favorite human cartoon characters. Why not try making cartoon drawings of your friends and family? Or find a newspaper picture of a famous person and make a cartoon "portrait" of him or her. You can also have fun making up your own imaginary cartoon character. Or draw cartoon faces with different expressions – happy, sad, angry, or frightened. You will get lots of ideas by looking at cartoons in books and newspapers, and by observing people around you.

To create a funny cartoon figure, pick out one or two obvious features, such as a large nose or an unusual hairstyle and exaggerate them – in a friendly way, of course! Here are some ideas to get you started . . .

Look at the different expressions you can capture with just a line for a mouth and dots for eyes.

A downward mouth and squinted eyes show an angry person.

Miss Prim. The cartoonist has given her a long face and no chin, glasses, a funny hairdo, a pointed nose, and a prim little mouth.

An upward mouth and raised eyebrows show a happy person.

Here's the retired officer, still barking out his orders. See how his open mouth is exaggerated.

Cartoon children usually have freckles, big ears, and messy hair!

Exaggerate people's shapes for a humorous effect. In cartoons, tall, thin people have stretched-out heads and necks and long, skinny arms and legs. Short, fat people have round heads and no neck, short legs, and big bellies.

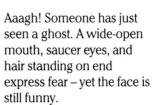

Aaagh! Someone has just seen a ghost. A wide-open mouth, saucer eyes, and hair standing on end express fear – yet the face is still funny.

25

Measuring the body

When you draw or paint a picture of someone, do you sometimes find that you have made the head too big, or the legs too short, or the hands too small? If you want your pictures of people to look realistic, you have to get all the different parts of the body in correct *proportion*. At first you may think this is very hard – no two bodies are exactly the same. What's more, the younger someone is, the bigger the head is in relation to the rest of the body. Luckily, whether a person is young or old, short or tall, or fat or thin, there are some simple rules to help you get different parts of the body looking right and in proportion to each other.

In babies, the head goes about 4 times into the height of the body.

In older children, the head goes about 6 times into the height of the body.

When the arms are stretched out, the length from the fingertips of one hand to the fingertips of the other hand is equal to the height of the body.

Adult proportions

In adults, the head goes about 7 times into the height of the body.

The elbow comes about halfway down the arm.

The legs start about halfway down the body.

When the arms hang at the sides, the tips of the fingers reach down to halfway between the hips and the knees.

The knees are about halfway down the legs.

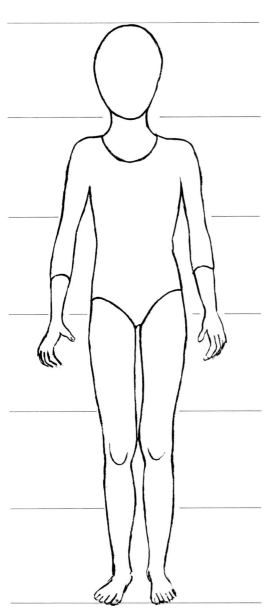

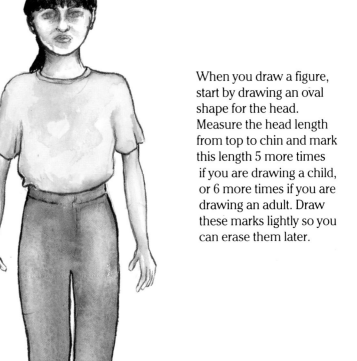

When you draw a figure, start by drawing an oval shape for the head. Measure the head length from top to chin and mark this length 5 more times if you are drawing a child, or 6 more times if you are drawing an adult. Draw these marks lightly so you can erase them later.

Heads you win!

The head-measuring method is a good way to check that your drawing will fit on the page. If you don't measure, you might reach the bottom of the page before you finish your drawing. Seth, aged 11, drew these two pictures. Guess which one used the "head-measuring" method!

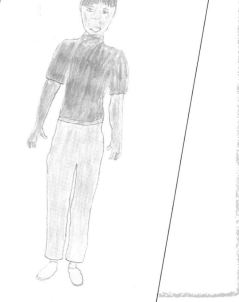

The human body comes in all sizes and shapes. Just look around you – some people are fat, some are tall and skinny, some are short. Everybody looks different, but the proportions of the body are nearly always about the same.

Drawing the body

The human body is made up of many complicated shapes, so it is easier to draw if you start with soft pencil guidelines, breaking it down into simple shapes first. Think of the body as being made up of little scraps – rather like the Tin Man from the film *The Wizard of Oz*. The head is shaped like an egg, the arms and legs like sausages, and so on. Following the steps below, you can make your own "Tin Man." When you have completed your "Tin Man" drawing, you can start to build up the different parts of the body in more detail to make your picture more realistic.

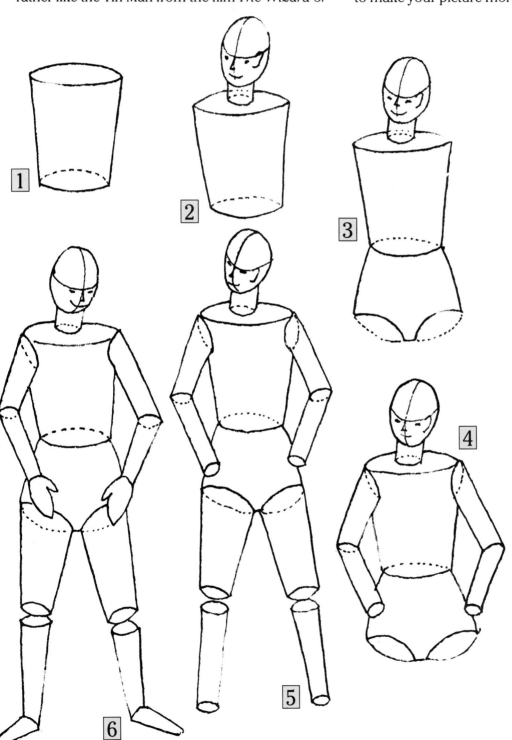

1 The chest is shaped like a bucket.

2 Add on an egg shape for the head and a tin can for the neck.

3 The stomach and hips are shaped like a pair of shorts.

4 The arms are like sausages joined in the middle.

5 The tops of the legs are like cardboard rolls, but fatter at the top than at the bottom. The bottoms of the legs are the same, but thinner. The knees are round like tennis balls.

6 Add simple mitten shapes for the hands and wedges for the feet.

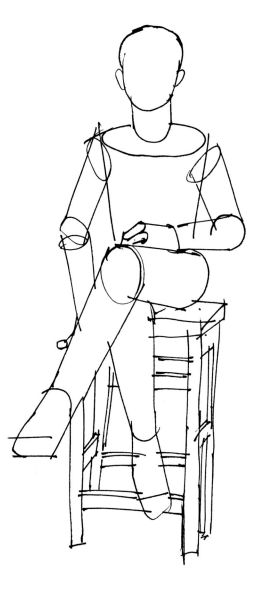

The "Tin Man" method works especially well when you are drawing people in complicated poses. It helps you to see the positions of the limbs more clearly.

Using the simple drawing as a guide, you can now start to draw your model's clothes. The artist has done this in the picture on the right.

When the drawing is finished, rub out the guidelines.

Now try drawing some "Tin Men" of your own in lots of different poses.

People moving

Drawing people who are moving may seem difficult at first. But it's like learning to ride a bike – the more you practice, the easier it becomes. And moving figures can make your pictures really exciting!

Before starting to draw a moving figure, spend some time just sitting and watching. Concentrate all your attention on the action of the figure, and how the legs, arms, head, and back are positioned. Notice how the balance of the body changes during the action. Perform the action yourself if it helps. Now try a lot of quick sketches. Don't worry about mistakes – the important thing is to catch the shape and expression of the body.

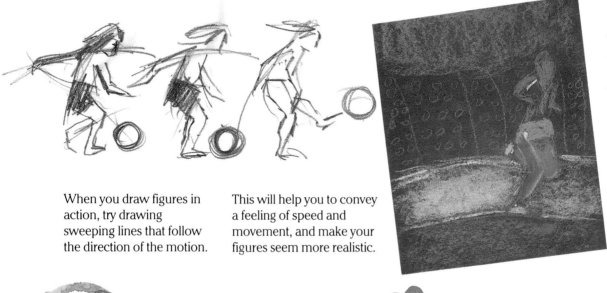

When you draw figures in action, try drawing sweeping lines that follow the direction of the motion. This will help you to convey a feeling of speed and movement, and make your figures seem more realistic.

Nikki, aged 8, made this chalk drawing of a runner. He looks as if he is going to sprint right off the page!

Make a flick book

To make a flick book, you will need a small notebook and a pen or pencil. The idea is to make small sketches of a moving figure on the corners of the pages, then flick the pages very fast to make the figure "move."

Make your first sketch in the bottom corner of the last page – not the first page – of your notebook. Make your second sketch in the bottom corner of the page before that, and so on until the movement is completed.

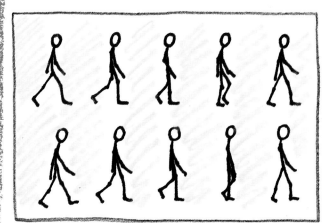

Lift up the pages at the corner with your thumb and rapidly flick them. As you do this, your figure will appear to "walk." This is similar to the way in which cartoon films are made.

Get a friend to repeat a simple movement such as walking. At several points during the action, ask him or her to stop and hold the pose while you make quick "pin man" sketches.

Sports fields and dance classes are good places to go to draw moving figures. Dancers and sports players repeat the same actions again and again. This makes it easier to record the movements.

33

Scribble drawing

T ake your sketchbook along to a sports center or ice rink and make lots of speedy scribble drawings of figures in action. Try to catch the actions and poses with just two or three strokes of your pencil. The drawings don't have to be accurate. You are not drawing the people, but what they are *doing*.

Use your whole arm as you draw, not just your fingers and wrist, and make fast, loose strokes. Keep your pencil moving all the time, hardly ever lifting it from the paper. Can you see how the scribbled lines give a feeling of movement to the figures?

These scribbled drawings were made at a soccer game. When you try "scribble drawing," why not try drawing without looking at the paper. This can help you to look carefully at the person you're drawing – and you might be surprised at the results!

This sketch of a girl dancing was made very quickly. When you have practised the "scribble drawing" method you will find it much easier to capture a feeling of movement in your pictures.

Felt-tip pens are great for doing scribble drawings. They make you draw fast and free because you can't rub out mistakes!

Expressions

Y ou know what sort of mood someone is in by the expression on their face. Every day you will see all sorts of expressions – happy, sad, excited, bored, angry, surprised or afraid. The best way to learn to draw expressions is by making faces in a mirror and watching how your mouth, eyes, eyebrows and cheeks change shape as you change expression.

When you are worried, your face looks long. Your mouth and eyes droop and look sad.

Here's an angry face. This man looks like a snarling dog!

This is a jealous face. The mouth and eyes are mean.

When you laugh, the corners of your mouth turn up.

When you are afraid, your mouth gets small and tight, and your eyes widen.

When you are surprised, your mouth drops open, your eyes open wide and your eyebrows shoot up.

Making faces
Look at these six different faces. Can you describe the feeling each one expresses? Choose two different faces and see if you can copy them. Use pencils, paints or crayons. Both the eyes and the mouth show a person's mood. Cover up the eyes on each photo – you can still tell the person's mood by looking at the mouth.

Body language

It is not just the face that expresses someone's mood or personality – so does the body. When people are happy or excited they jump around and wave their arms in the air. When they are angry they may stand with legs apart, head thrust forward and hands on hips. When they are sad their head is bowed and their shoulders droop. Body and face expressions make your paintings of people come to life.

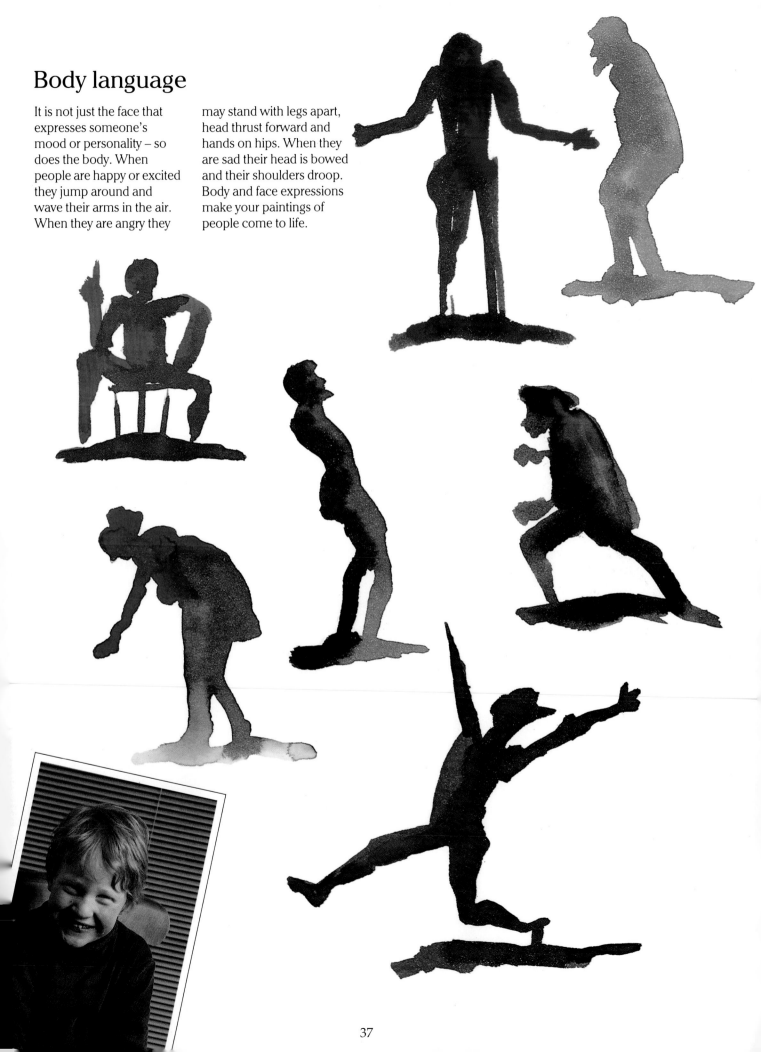

Hands up!

Hands are bigger than you might think. Look in a mirror and hold your hand up in front of your face, with your wrist resting on your chin. You will see that, from the wrist to the fingertips, your hand is almost as long as your face and about half as wide.

Hands seem difficult to draw at first because they are a funny shape. Three main shapes make up the hand. They are the thumb, the fingers and the palm area. Begin by drawing these sections as simple shapes, as shown on the right. Once you have drawn these shapes, you can start to add more details and shading to make them look more realistic.

1 Start with a circle for the palm.

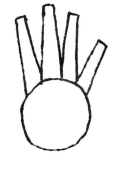

2 Add on the fingers (notice that the middle finger is the longest).

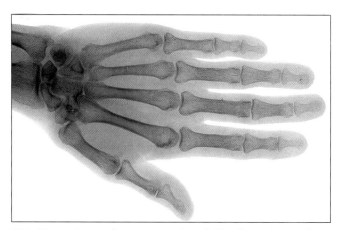

This X-ray picture shows the bone structure of the hand. The finger bones fan out from the wrist.

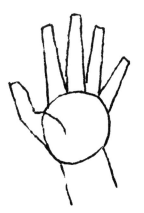

3 Add on the thumb. It is much shorter than the other fingers.

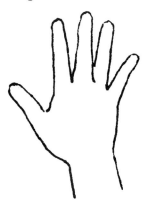

4 Now draw the hand and finger shapes properly and rub out your pencil guidelines.

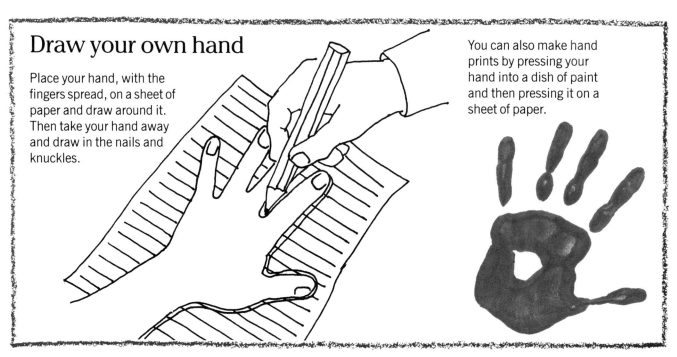

Draw your own hand

Place your hand, with the fingers spread, on a sheet of paper and draw around it. Then take your hand away and draw in the nails and knuckles.

You can also make hand prints by pressing your hand into a dish of paint and then pressing it on a sheet of paper.

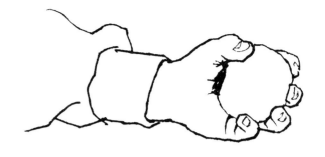

Ask your friends or family to keep their hands still for you while they are reading or watching TV. Draw as many different hands as you can – men's hands, women's hands, old hands, young hands, and so on. Or practice drawing your own hand, stretched out or clenched into a fist. After some practice, see if you can draw hands holding a book, or sewing.

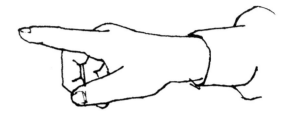

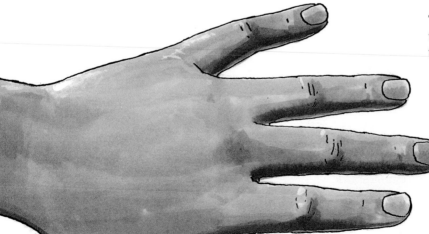

The fingers taper toward the ends, but widen out at the joints.

The fingers are about half the length of the whole hand.

Look at the shapes in between the fingers – it helps you to get the shapes of the fingers right.

The width across the knuckles is about the same as the length of the fingers.

The fingers have two joints but the thumb only has one.

Feet First

W e don't take much notice of our feet, probably because they are usually hidden inside shoes and socks. But when you draw and paint people, it is important to know how to draw both bare feet and feet wearing shoes.

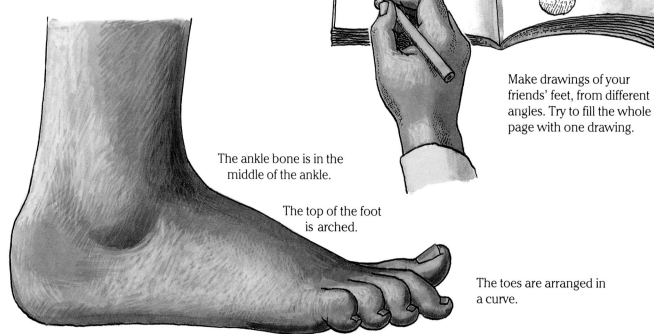

Make drawings of your friends' feet, from different angles. Try to fill the whole page with one drawing.

A foot seen from the side

The ankle bone is in the middle of the ankle.

The top of the foot is arched.

The toes are arranged in a curve.

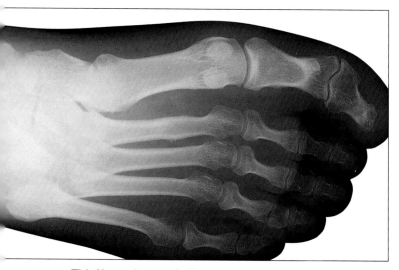

This X-ray picture of a foot shows how many small bones it contains.

A foot seen from the front

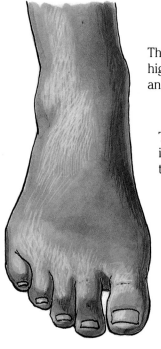

The inside ankle bone is higher than the outside ankle bone.

The foot looks shorter than it does when we see it from the side.

The big toe has only one joint. The others have two.

The ends of the toes have rounded pads.

Shoes come in all shapes and sizes. Here are just a few. How many other kinds can you think of?

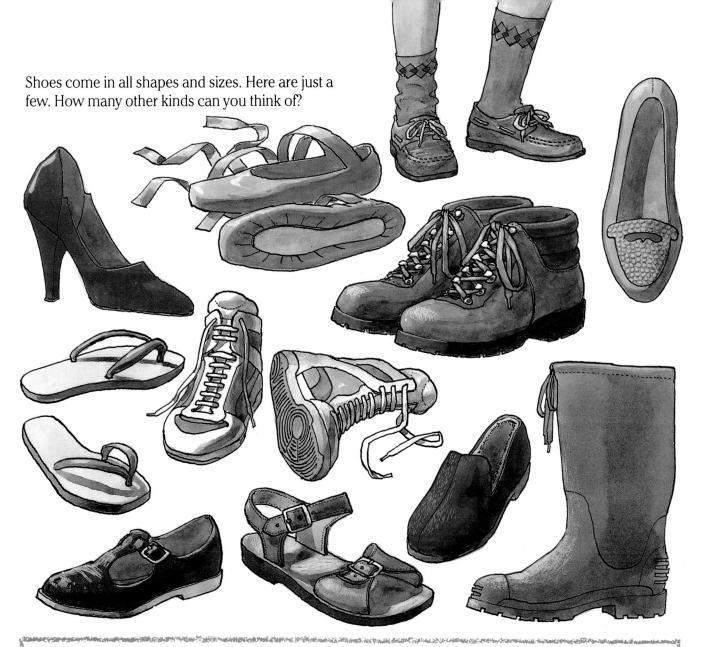

Foot prints

If you look at the soles of boots and sports shoes, you will see that they have interesting raised patterns, called treads. You can use these patterns to make foot prints.

Get a friend to wear a pair of boots or sports shoes and stand on a sheet of cardboard or stiff paper. Draw around the edge of the shoes; then cut out the shapes.

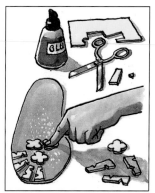

Using scraps of things such as corrugated cardboard, string, cork, or plastic foam, copy the shapes of the raised patterns on the soles. Then glue them onto the sole shapes.

Brush the raised patterns with poster paint and make prints on paper. See how many different patterns you can collect.

41

Pencils

A pencil and a sheet of paper are all you need to start drawing. Artists like to have plenty of pencils, which they use for making quick sketches as well as detailed drawings. Pencils are great "thinking sticks." With a pencil in your hand, you can put down on paper all those brilliant ideas you have in your head!

Take a large piece of paper and try doing some doodles with your pencils. Draw circles, squiggles, straight lines and crisscross lines. Press hard with the pencil, then press lightly. Try out different kinds of paper, too: some papers, such as brown parcel paper, have interesting textures that show through when you rub over them with the side of the pencil.

Arty says...
When you draw, hold your pencil farther away from the point than you do when you are writing. This will give you more freedom of movement.

Try drawing lines at different speeds. Make fast, zigzag lines, slow, wavy lines and so on. Do you see how these lines create different feelings?

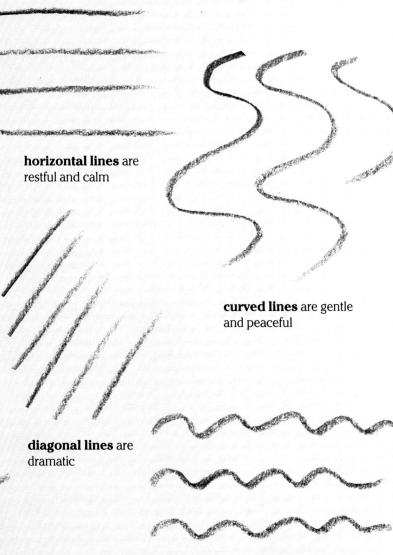

horizontal lines are restful and calm

radiating lines are happy, like the sun

diagonal lines are dramatic

curved lines are gentle and peaceful

zig-zag lines are active and energetic

wavy lines are fast, like a stream flowing over rocks

Make a copy of this drawing and try out the different methods the artist used.

Use the pencil point to draw dots and dashes.

Diagonal lines that crisscross each other make interesting patterns. You can draw the lines close together or far apart.

These soft marks are made by rubbing with the side of a soft pencil. Smudge the marks with your fingertip to make them even softer.

Lots of diagonal lines drawn close together are called "hatching." This is good for shading.

Pencil leads come in different grades, from very hard to very soft. Hard pencils range from H to 12H (the hardest). Soft pencils range from B to 8B (the softest). HB and F are in between.

Soft pencils make broad, dark lines. They are also good for shading.

Hard pencils make thin, light lines. They are good for drawing details and patterns.

Erasers can be used for smudging pencil lines together as well as for rubbing out mistakes.

Pastels and colored pencils

Pastels and colored pencils are good for sketching outdoors because they are easy to carry and you don't need brushes and water to mix the colors.

Pastels are made from colored powder mixed with gum and rolled into sticks. There are hundreds of wonderful colors to choose from, but it is best to start off with just a few, or buy a boxed set. Pastels are soft and crumbly, so you can blend colors together on your paper by rubbing them with your fingertip. Use the point to make sharp lines. Snap a piece off the stick and use it on its side to fill in large areas. Pastel smudges easily, so keep your hand above the paper as you draw, and keep blowing away the dust.

Neopastels are similar to ordinary pastels, but the colors are stronger and they don't smudge.

Colored pencils also come in dozens of different colors, and you can buy sets in boxes. Their sharp points are good for drawing small details. You can also buy special watercolor pencils. With these, you can draw and paint at the same time! You draw with the pencil in the normal way, then brush over the lines with a brush and water. The color dissolves and you can spread it with your brush, just like paint.

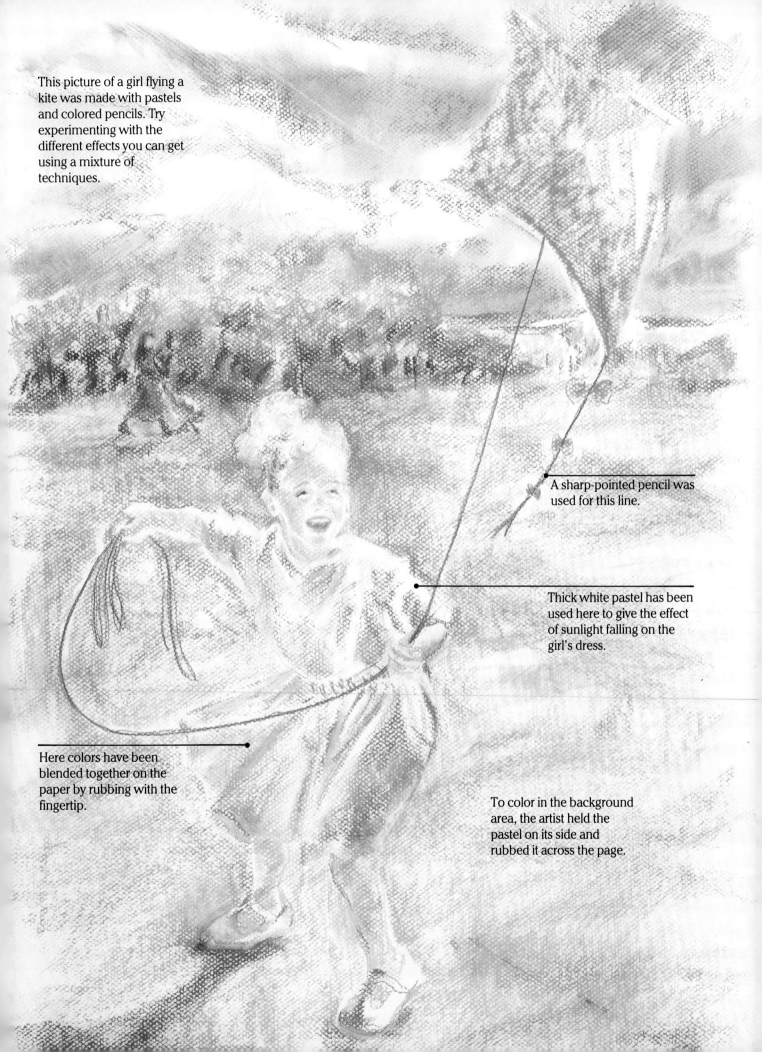

This picture of a girl flying a kite was made with pastels and colored pencils. Try experimenting with the different effects you can get using a mixture of techniques.

A sharp-pointed pencil was used for this line.

Thick white pastel has been used here to give the effect of sunlight falling on the girl's dress.

Here colors have been blended together on the paper by rubbing with the fingertip.

To color in the background area, the artist held the pastel on its side and rubbed it across the page.

Drawing yourself

I f you want to learn more about drawing portraits, a good way is to set up a mirror and draw yourself. As you don't have to ask someone else to pose for you, you can work on your drawing any time you like.

A dresser mirror is useful because you can rest your drawing board on the edge of the table and the mirror is just the right distance away from you. Settle yourself comfortably and make sure there is plenty of light to work in.

Try out different poses. Do you want to face the mirror, or sit slightly to one side? Do you want to include only your face, or your neck and shoulders as well?

Before you begin your portrait, look closely at your face in the mirror and make sketches of your features. What shape are your eyes? How far apart are they? Is your mouth big or small? Try out different expressions. As you change expression, watch how your eyes, eyebrows, cheeks and mouth move and change shape. By getting to know your face in this way, you will find it easier to draw a good likeness.

Rest your drawing board at an angle so you don't have to move your head too much when you look up from your drawing to the mirror.

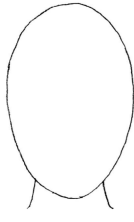

1

Start by drawing an egg shape for the face, and add the neck. Draw very lightly because you might want to make corrections later.

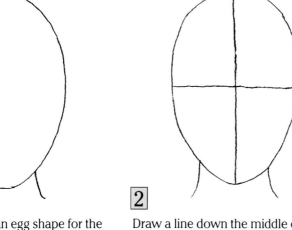

2

Draw a line down the middle of the head. This will help you to position the nose. Draw another line across the middle for the eyes to rest on.

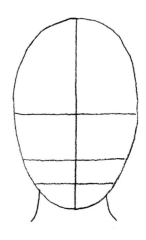

3

Draw a line halfway between the eye line and the chin where the tip of the nose will come. Draw another line between the nose line and the chin. This is where the mouth should go.

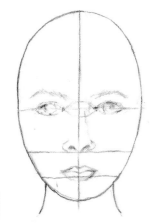

4

Draw rough shapes for the eyes, nose and mouth. Check that they are the right size and in the correct position. On most people, the eyes are about one eye-width apart.

5

Now you can start to fill in the details and draw the hair. Look for the areas of light and shadow. First shade in the light areas with light pencil lines.

6

Finally shade in the darkest areas. Don't forget to give your portrait a background.

Drawing with pens and markers

Have you tried using felt-tip pens, markers and ballpoint pens for drawing? Drawing with pens is good practice because it makes you work boldly – once you have made a mark on the paper it has to stay there. Don't be put off because you can't rub out your mistakes – just go over the lines again. Lines and wrinkles make faces more interesting – and the same goes for drawings!

Pens and markers come in hundreds of colors and a wide choice of pen points, from very fine to chunky, wedge-shaped tips.

Fine points are good for lines and details.

Bullet-shaped points make thicker lines and dots.

Wedge-shaped tips are useful for filling in areas of color. You can also use the edge of the point to make fine lines and graduated "italic" curves.

Rolling-ball pens are pleasant to draw with. They give lines of even width.

Ordinary ballpoint pens can be used in the same way, but they are not so smooth.

Drawing out and about

Felt-tips and pens are great for outdoor sketching because they are easy to carry around and you can draw very quickly with them. The colors dry quickly, and there are no brushes to clean.

Take a pocket notebook and pen with you when you are out and about. When you spot something interesting, make a quick sketch there and then. Here are some places where you will find plenty of people – and interesting backgrounds – to draw:

- The local park
- Trains and buses
- A trip to the store
- The zoo
- The amusement park
- The beach

Try combining different nib shapes and thicknesses in the same drawing. This picture shows some effects you can achieve with markers and pens.

You can apply one color over another to make interesting color mixtures. (The first color needs to be lighter than the second one.)

Markers can be used to color in shapes drawn in outline with a pen.

Make tiny dots with the nib. Lots of dots close together make dark areas. Fewer dots more spaced out make light areas. This method is called *pointillism*.

Patterns and textures are produced by making short strokes close together.

Loose, streaky effects can be made with a dried-up marker.

Arty says...
Always remember to replace the cap on felt-tips and marker pens when you are not using them. If not, the point will quickly dry out. (But keep your dried-up pens – they make streaky marks that are good for drawing tree bark, stone walls and grass.)

Light and shade

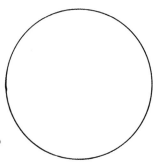

O ur bodies are not flat, like a pancake; they are solid and round. But when we paint and draw figures, how can we make them look solid and round on a flat sheet of paper? The answer is: by using light and shade. When light hits any object, it creates light parts and dark parts. The parts nearest to the light are the brightest. The parts facing away from the light are the darkest. By observing this in your drawings and paintings, you can make your figures look more lifelike.

This shape is a circle. On the page opposite, we have changed the circle into a ball, by adding shadows.

The face on the left looks flat, like a cartoon drawing. By adding shadows, we have made the figure look real and lifelike.

Drawing shadows

Shadows on the figure usually fade gradually from dark to light. Different ways of drawing shadows give different effects. Close or wide spacing on **hatching** or **cross-hatching** gives dark or light areas. Add interest to both with thick and thin lines, lines in different directions, or two or more colors. **Stipple** dots, widely or closely spaced, give light or dark areas. **Smudging** with your finger can evenly blend shadows from light to dark.

hatching (pen and ink, ballpoint pens, fiber-tip, stylo-pens)

smudging (chalk, crayon, soft pencil, charcoal)

cross-hatching (pen and ink, ballpoint, fiber-tip, stylo-pens)

stipple (stylo-pens, fiber-tip)

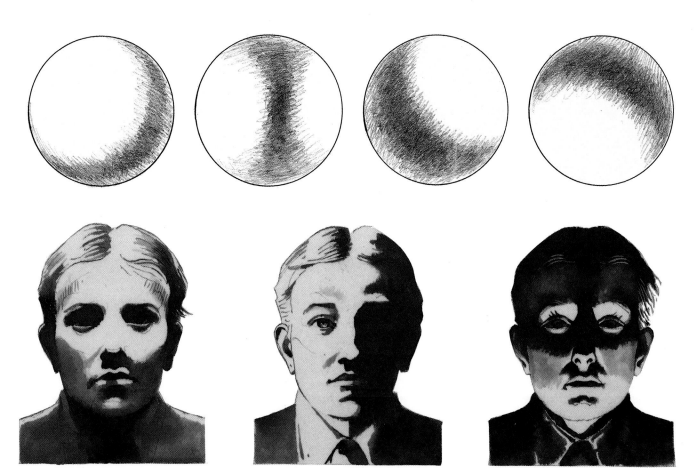

The light on this face comes from the left, just above the head. This sort of lighting is good for a natural sort of portrait with soft shadows.

This head is brightly lit from the side, giving strong contrast to shadows and highlights. This sort of lighting can add lots of drama to a portrait.

This head is brightly lit from under the chin and gives strong shadows. Although it gives weird and spooky effects, it is not very natural looking.

Cast Shadows

The shadows cast onto the ground by an object are important, too. Without them, your figures look as if they are floating in midair! The length of a cast shadow depends on the position of the sun in the sky.

Remember that shadows always fall in the opposite direction to where the sun is shining from. Look at these two pictures: can you tell where the sun is?

When the sun is high in the sky, the shadow is short.

When the sun is low in the sky, the shadow is long.

Torn paper pictures

This project is fun to do and will help you to observe the patterns of light and shadow on your subject and to copy them. The idea is to look at the colors in your subject and decide how light or dark they are. For instance, your sweater might be dark red, but in bright sunshine some parts of the sweater will look much lighter than others, because the light shines brightly on some parts and makes dark shadows on other parts.

Arty says...
Try squinting when you look at your subject. This makes it easier to see the contrast between light areas and dark areas.

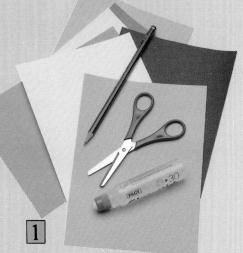

1 Start by collecting sheets of black, white and gray paper. Newspaper works well. You will also need scissors, glue and a sheet of paper.

2 Find a magazine photo of a face with strong light and dark contrasts.

3 On a large sheet of paper, copy or trace the outline of the face only.

4 Now look for all the light areas and all the dark areas on the face. Copy the shapes of these light and dark areas onto your drawing, as if you were drawing a map or completing a jigsaw.

5 Now decide which are the darkest areas, the lightest areas, and the areas that are in between light and dark. Make a "collage" of the face from torn paper. Take your piece of black paper and tear it into shapes that fit the areas of dark color on the photograph (they don't have to be exact). Glue the shapes in place.

6 Do the same with torn pieces of white paper, and glue them onto the areas of lightest color.

7 Finally, do the same with pieces of gray paper, gluing them to the shapes you decided were in between the lightest and the darkest. You should now have a black and white version of the original colored photograph!

Mixing colors

When you decide to paint something, you must look carefully at the subject and try to see all the different colors and shades within it. Then you have to know how to mix the colors you see in it using the paints you have. It is important to learn how paints mix, because it will help make your paintings more realistic. It also saves you money, because from just a few tubes of paint, you can make many different shades and tones, simply by mixing different colors together. These pages will show you how to mix paints to get all the colors you need.

A rainbow is made up of seven colors: red, orange, yellow, green, blue, indigo (dark blue), and violet (purple), in that order. All the colors you see around you are made from these colors.

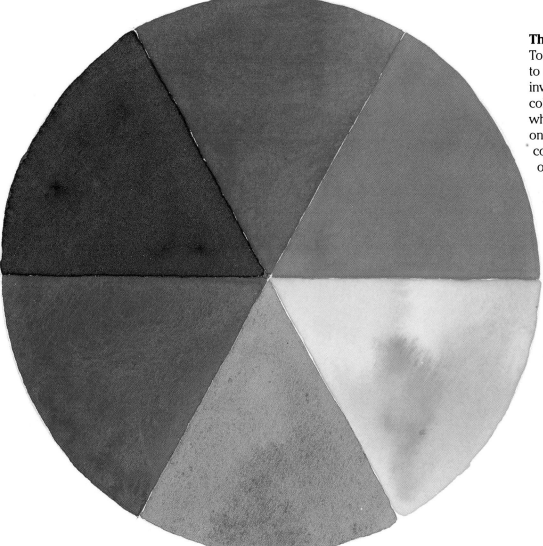

The color wheel
To make color mixing easy to understand, artists invented an idea called the color wheel. The color wheel is like a rainbow, only made into a circle. The colors are in the same order as they appear in a rainbow. You can make your own color wheel using watercolors (poster paints don't work very well for color mixing). Draw a circle, and divide it into six equal sections. Color the sections red, orange, yellow, green, blue, and violet (purple).

Looking at your color wheel, you will make some interesting discoveries about color mixing.

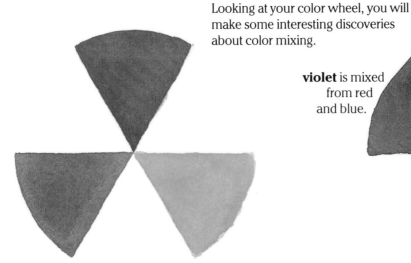

violet is mixed from red and blue.

orange is mixed from red and yellow.

green is mixed from yellow and blue.

Primary colors Red, yellow, and blue cannot be mixed from other colors. They are called *primary colors*.

Secondary colors These colors are made by mixing any two primary colors together.

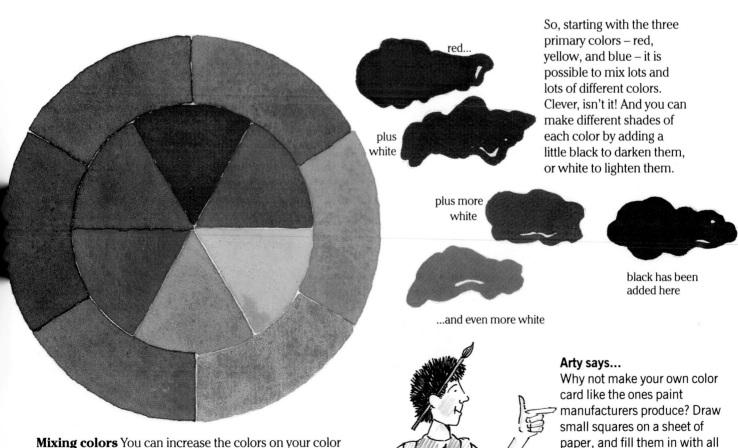

red...

plus white

plus more white

...and even more white

black has been added here

So, starting with the three primary colors – red, yellow, and blue – it is possible to mix lots and lots of different colors. Clever, isn't it! And you can make different shades of each color by adding a little black to darken them, or white to lighten them.

Mixing colors You can increase the colors on your color wheel to twelve, by mixing together any two colors that lie next to each other on the six-color wheel. This gives you what are called *tertiary colors* (pronounced "ter-shary"), which are red-orange, yellow-orange, yellow-green, blue-green, blue-violet, and red-violet.

Arty says...
Why not make your own color card like the ones paint manufacturers produce? Draw small squares on a sheet of paper, and fill them in with all the exciting colors you have mixed. Give each color an appropriate and descriptive name, such as "rebellion red," or "soggy cabbage green."

When you have discovered how to mix colors that are next to each other on the color wheel, try using colors that are opposite each other on the wheel.

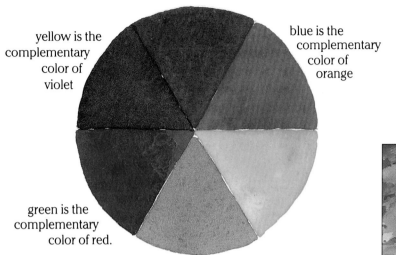

yellow is the complementary color of violet

blue is the complementary color of orange

green is the complementary color of red.

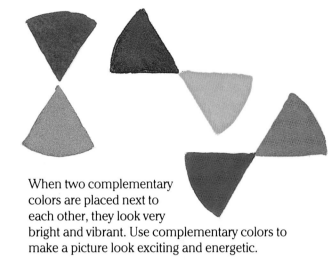

When two complementary colors are placed next to each other, they look very bright and vibrant. Use complementary colors to make a picture look exciting and energetic.

Complementary colors Colors opposite each other on the color wheel are called *complementary colors*. Green is the complementary color of red; blue is the complementary of orange, and yellow is the complementary of violet. Notice that each primary color is always opposite a secondary color. It is never opposite another primary color.

red
yellow
mixture
blue

green
mixture
red

mixture
violet
yellow

orange
yellow
green
mixture

Grays and browns Mixing black and white is only one way of making gray. You can make much more interesting and varied grays by mixing together varying amounts of the primary colors – red, yellow, and blue. Or you can mix grays and browns by using two complementary colors.

Warm and cool colors

The color wheel shows that colors can be divided into two types – warm and cool. On one side are the warm colors – the reds, oranges, and yellows of fire. On the other side are the cool colors – the blues and greens of grass and water. Warm and cool colors play an important part in paintings. For example, in a portrait, the shadows are usually dark and cool, containing grays, blues, and greens. The parts of the figure exposed to the light are brighter and warmer in color.

The paintings on the left and right are by the same artist. However, each one has a very different feel because the different types of colors used by the artist. The painting of three children on the beach (on the left) is painted mainly in warm yellows and oranges (with splashes of their complementary colors violet and blue) to give the feeling of a hot summer day. The picture on the right, called "It's freezing," *looks* freezing because it was painted mainly in cool blues and blue-greens.

Make a Color Scrapbook

Keep scraps of colored paper, fabric, and candy wrappers to make a color scrapbook. See how many different kinds of each color you can collect. Label the colors "warm," "cool," "bright," "pale," and so on.

Painting with only a few colors

It is tempting to use lots of different colors when you paint a picture. But why not challenge yourself sometimes, and paint a picture using just a few colors? It's a good way to learn about colors and what happens to them when you mix them together.

If you've read page 53, you will know that it is possible to create a wide range of colors by mixing the three primary colors – red, yellow, and blue – to make secondary and tertiary colors. As a project, try painting a portrait or figure using just three colors plus white. The portrait on the opposite page was painted this way, and it is very lifelike.

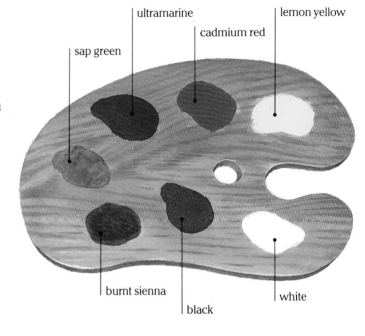

sap green
ultramarine
cadmium red
lemon yellow
burnt sienna
black
white

Arty says...
Use a piece of scrap paper to test colors before putting them on your painting. You can test your color-mixing skills by trying to mix a color to match a piece of colored paper.

Instead of spending your money on dozens of tubes of cheap paint, buy five or six tubes of good-quality paint in useful colors – you will get far better results. Here is a list of recommended colors:

- Lemon yellow
- Cadmium red
- Ultramarine (a warm blue)
- Sap green
- Burnt sienna (a warm brown)
- Black
- White

Painting with one color

See if you can make a painting using only one color. Choose any color you like, and mix three different shades of it in separate dishes. Make a dark, a light, and a medium shade.

For the dark shade, mix the color with a little black. For the light shade, mix the color with a little white. For the medium shade, mix the color with just a little water. Use your color to paint the light, dark, and medium areas in your subject.

As you can see, painting with only one color can be very effective. It gives a strong impression of light and shade.

These are the colors the artist started with:

These are the colors that were mixed from the original colors. Some colors were mixed with white to make them lighter. Some colors were mixed with black to make them darker.

Painting skin

What color is skin? We might say that skin is "brown" or "white" or "pink" or "black." But when we look closely, we can see all sorts of colors in our skin – including gray, green, and blue! This is because skin reflects the colors around it. Test this for yourself by looking at the back of your hand in bright sunlight and then in shadow – see how the color of your skin appears to change? Look especially at the shadowy parts – do they sometimes look bluish or greenish? Next time you paint people, think about how you can mix your colors to make the skin look more realistic. These pages give you some tips.

1

Arty says...
Mix some paint, and see if you can match it to your own skin color. Test your mixture by dabbing some paint onto the back of your hand to see how closely it matches. Below are some blobs of paint of different skin colors.

Look for the light and dark parts of the skin – the highlights and shadows – and mix light and dark colors for each. This is how artists make their figures look real, as if we could reach out and touch them. Usually the parts that stick out, like the nose and forehead, are lighter, and the parts that go in, like the hollow under the bottom lip, are darker.

1 For this portrait, the artist first of all filled in the main areas of shadow, using blocks of dark color. The picture has been painted on colored paper, rather than white, which gives an interesting effect.
2 Next, some details were painted in and more highlights added with white paint.

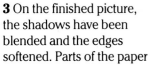

3 On the finished picture, the shadows have been blended and the edges softened. Parts of the paper have been left to show through on some of the lighter parts of the face.

Right and wrong

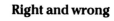

☒ If you add black to make skin darker in the shadow parts, the color looks muddy and dead.

☑ Instead, try adding a small touch of brown, blue, or green to the basic skin color for the shadow parts. You'll find it looks more realistic.

Skin color

Some people have very light skin, some have very dark skin, and others are somewhere in between. Here are three portraits of people from different ethnic backgrounds – see how the artist has used different color mixtures to paint each one.

Mixtures of brown, gray, blue and violet were used for this portrait. Black was used for the hair – but not for the skin.

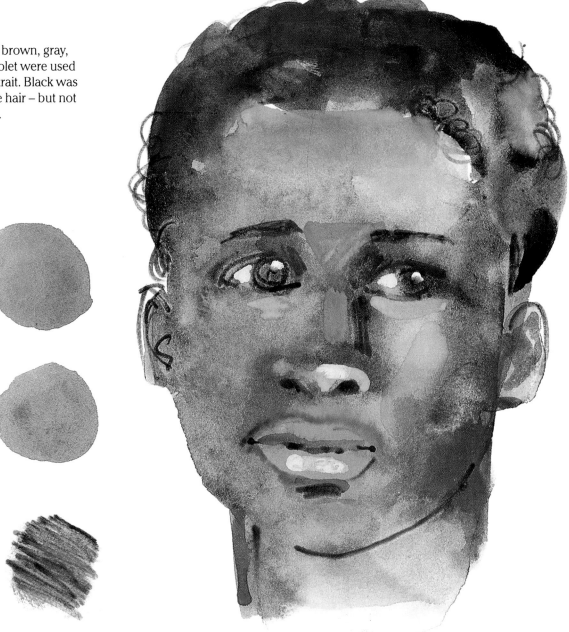

This girl has pale skin. The artist used yellow, pink and brown, and left some areas white, to model the shape of her face.

This man might be Asian or Latin American. His skin is a dark, warm brown. Notice how the artist has modeled the face with patches of dark brown, orange- brown and pinkish-brown. There are touches of green and blue, too, where the shiny parts of the skin reflect the colors around it.

Hair

When you are drawing hair, it is not a good idea to try to draw separate strands. This makes your subjects look as if they have spaghetti sprouting out of their heads! For a better effect, start by drawing the outline shape of the hair, then make a few lines and strokes in the same direction as the hair grows. Short curls can be drawn with groups of C-shaped strokes. Draw wavy hair with S-shaped strokes.

Notice the areas of light and shade on the hair (squint at them to see them better). The top of the hair is usually lighter, because light shines on it from above. The hair on one side of the head may be lighter if it faces the direction of the light.

If you are painting shiny hair, try leaving small areas of the white paper unpainted to show the highlights (see the girl in the blue sweater at the bottom of the next page).

Always use light, feathery strokes with your pencil or brush. If you press too hard, the hair will look solid and hard instead of soft.

Hair comes in many different styles – long and short, straight and curly, wavy and spiky. People's hairstyles help us to identify who they are. Men sometimes have beards, moustaches and bushy eyebrows, too. Here are some examples of different hairstyles – see how many you can spot next time you are out and about.

These pictures show step-by-step how to paint hair seen from the front and from the side.

Paint the head first. Make sure you get the proportions right. Then paint the outline of the hair.

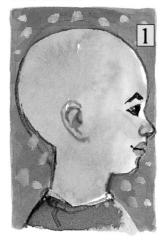

There are several different methods you can use to express the texture of hair. Some of them are shown below.

Let the paint dry. Finally, add a few thin strokes with the tip of your brush.

While the paint is still damp, scratch into it with the end of your brush to indicate a few strands here and there.

Wipe most of the paint off your brush; then skim the brush lightly over the paper. This makes feathery, broken strokes that look like strands of hair.

Apply a thin wash of color. When it is dry, make light strokes over it with colored pencils.

Strokes of pastel or charcoal can be softly blended together with your finger.

With watercolor, you can paint one wash of color over another while the first is still damp. The colors mix together to create a soft effect.

Apply strokes of wax crayon and then scratch out some lines with a sharp point to indicate a few strands.

How to draw and paint clothes

When you draw and paint people, pay special attention to the clothes they are wearing. Clothes usually follow the shape of the body, so if you draw them correctly they can help you to make the figure look rounded instead of flat. For example, the collar of a shirt follows the round shape of the neck, the sleeves of a dress wrap around the arms, the tops of socks wrap around the legs, and a belt wraps around the waist.

Look at the patterns on clothing, too. The lines of stripes and checks are not always straight – they bend where they wrap around arms and legs.

The folds and creases in clothes indicate how the body is moving. In this picture of a skipping girl, see how the folds in her dress give a feeling of the skirt swinging as she jumps up and down.

Costumes Ask your friends to dress up in costumes and pose for you while you paint them.

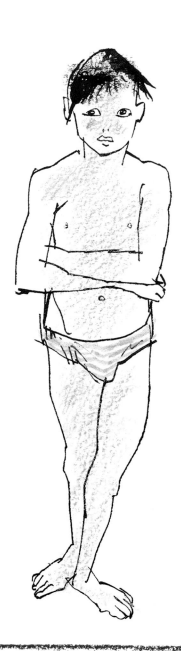

Putting on clothes
Look at the way the clothes
have been drawn in this
picture.

The hat band and brim
follow the round shape of
the head.

The collar follows the round
shape of the neck.

The jacket sleeves crease up
at the bend of the elbow.

Don't forget details such as
buttons, pocket flaps and so
on to make your drawing
realistic.

Note how the pattern of the
pants follows the rounded
forms of the legs.

Prints and patterns

Collect scraps of fabric in
different patterns and
colors. See how many
patterns you can find –
checks, stripes, flowers,
spots and dots and so on.
Draw squares on a sheet of
paper and fill them in with
your patterns – like the ones
shown here.

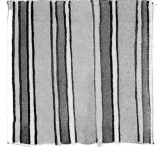
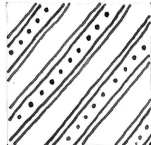

In the 18th century, rich men and women wore very elaborate clothes made from fine materials such as silk, satin, and lace. This is of a French lady, Madame de Pompadour. Why not make a copy of this painting, or collect pieces of paper or fabric and make a collage?

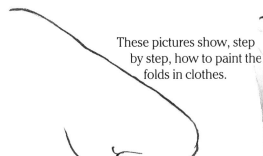

These pictures show, step by step, how to paint the folds in clothes.

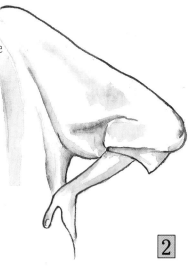

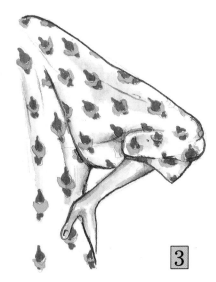

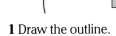
1 Draw the outline.

2 Draw the biggest folds and paint the shadows (don't make them too dark).

3 When the paint is dry, add the pattern of the fabric. See how the folds make the patterns stretch and bend.

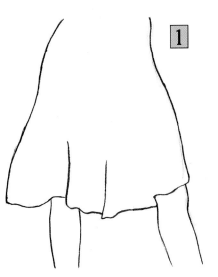

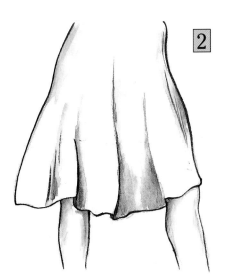

The stripes follow the form of the bow.

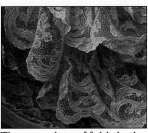

There are lots of folds in the lace of her sleeve.

These close-ups, taken from the portrait on the opposite page, show how the artist has carefully painted Madame de Pompadour's clothes. The fabric of the skirt looks smooth and shiny.

In this close-up, see how the light and shade on the sleeve shows the roundness of her arm.

Using paints

There are lots of different kinds of paint to choose from. Some come in bottles, some in tins, some in tubes. It is worth buying good-quality paints as they last longer and the colors are stronger.

Powder paints are cheap to buy, but you have to mix them with water before you can use them. Put some powder into a dish or jar and add the water a little at a time. The paint should be thick and creamy. If it is too runny, your paintings will look dull and wishy-washy.

Poster paints come in jars. They are runny, but quite thick. Poster paints are brightly colored, and they are more shiny than powder paints.

Watercolors come in small blocks. You wet your brush with water and rub it over the block to pick up the paint. Watercolor paint is much thinner and runnier than powder paints and poster paints. Always use white paper with watercolors.

Experiment with your paints to see what you can do with them. You can mix colors together on a palette, or you can mix them on the paper by letting two colors run together while they are wet. Try pressing objects such as sponges, leaves or bits of rough cloth into the wet paint to create textures.

Always replace the lids on your paints when you have finished, so they don't dry out. And always wash your brushes after you have used them; otherwise, the paint will clog up the hairs. Store your brushes with the bristles upward in an empty pot or jar.

Paints can be mixed with plenty of water to make them thin. Because the paint is runny, you can do lots of interesting things with it. This picture was painted with watercolors.

This interesting color mixture was made by letting three different colors run into each other while they were still wet.

With thin paint and the tip of a small brush, you can "draw" lines.

To show light and shadow on objects, first paint the light parts. Mix the paint with plenty of water. When the paint is dry, paint the shaded parts with a darker shade made by using more paint and less water.

Paint like the Impressionists!

On Page 53 we described how to mix two colors together to make a third color. Here is another way of color "mixing," called broken color. Instead of mixing two colors together with a brush, you apply separate strokes or dabs of one color, leaving spaces between them. Then you fill in the spaces with the other color. It's a bit like making a mosaic. From a distance, the two colors seem to merge together and make a third color. For example, you can make green from dabs, spots or strokes of blue and yellow.

The French Impressionist painters used broken color all the time because it gives a more interesting effect than flat, mixed color.

Start by making strokes with your first color. Leave spaces between the strokes.

When the first color is dry, fill in the spaces with your second color. Always wash your brush between colors. You can let the strokes overlap if you like.

You can apply your colors in lots of different ways. Try making tiny dots like these...

... or big, bold slabs of color.

Broken color works well with felt-tip pens, crayons and pastels, too. Try making a "broken color" picture using these different techniques.

Dots, dabs and dribbles of color were used to make this picture of a woman sewing. Colors applied in this way appear very lively and vibrant.

This portrait was painted in 1905 by a French artist, André Derain. It is of his friend Henri Matisse, who was also an artist. Derain painted the face with big blocks of color, like a mosaic. See how he used warm yellows and reds on one side of the face, where the light hits it. On the other side, where the face is in shadow, he used cool blues. Using poster paints or wax crayons, try making a copy of Derain's portrait.

Spitting images

When you draw or paint someone's portrait, your aim is to make your picture look as much like that person as possible. If you do a portrait of your friend Tim, and your other friends say "Wow, that's the spitting image of Tim!" you can feel very proud of yourself, because getting a good likeness of someone is not easy!

So what is the secret? Before you begin drawing, take a good long look at your model. What do you notice first about him or her? Is it the hair, the eyes or the mouth? How long is the hair, and exactly what color is it? Is the face long and thin, or is it round? Are the eyes large or small? What shape is the nose? Is the mouth wide, or small and button-like? Does your model have freckles? These are the kinds of questions you should ask yourself; look at each individual feature carefully before you draw it.

You might like to start by drawing the shape of the face first. Or you might prefer to draw the eyes, nose and mouth and then draw the face around it. Keep looking back at your model while you draw, and keep checking all the time that you have got the shapes right and the features in the correct position.

Below are paintings of six different children. What are the most noticeable features of each one? (Answers below each picture.)

Blond curly hair, dark eyes and freckles. Wearing a green turtleneck sweater.

Dark hair, blue eyes and a red nose. Wearing a red scarf, tied cowboy-style.

Black curly hair and freckled red cheeks. Wearing blue-rimmed glasses and a shirt and tie.

74

Things like jewelry and hats can help make your portraits look more interesting.

Two friends made drawings of each other in class. On the left is a portrait of Emma, drawn by Alexandra, aged 10. On the right is a portrait of Alexandra, drawn by Emma, also aged 10.

Dark hair tied in pigtails with blue bows, and a freckled nose. Wearing gold earrings and a dress with a collar.

Dark curly hair, heavy eyebrows and bright blue eyes. Wearing a dress with a ruffled collar.

Long red hair and lots of freckles. Wearing red beads and a red headband.

What is a portrait?

A portrait is a very special kind of painting. A really good portrait not only looks like the person being painted, it also tells us something about what kind of person they are, what kind of clothes they like to wear, and what their interests are. A portrait tells a story about the person you are painting – a story told in one picture, without words.

Try painting a portrait of someone you know well. Look at your model and ask yourself "What is it that makes this person special? How can I show this in my painting?" Think about how you can include objects in the picture that tell us something about the person and make the picture more interesting. For instance, if you are painting your mom, and she likes gardening, why not paint a portrait of her in the garden, surrounded by her favorite flowers?

Finnian Brigham, aged 10

Heather Sygrove, aged 11

Family portraits
These "family portraits" are all very different. Try and guess what sort of personalities these people might have. Then make a portrait of your family or friends. Try and think about expression and "body language" (see pages 34 and 35), as well as including objects which tell us more about the people in the picture.

Emma Appleby, aged 9

The portrait shown here was painted by an artist called Jan Van Eyck in the 15th century. It is called "The Arnolfini Marriage" and depicts an Italian merchant and his bride. The picture shows the marriage actually taking place in their own home.

The scene is reflected in the mirror on the back wall. We can also see two other people who have entered the room.

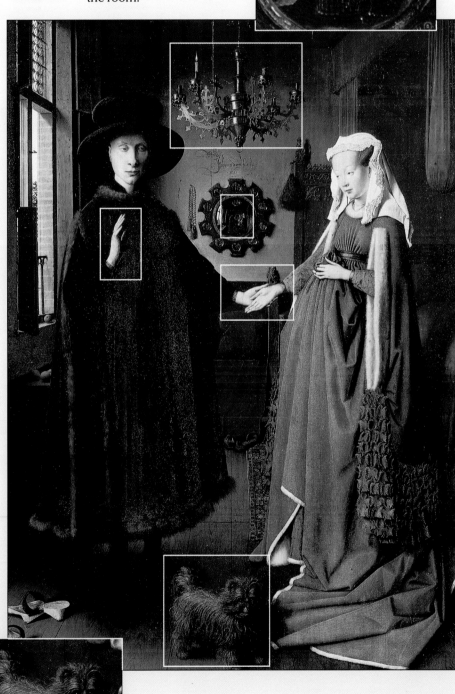

The single candle in the chandelier is a marriage candle.

The couple are holding hands.

The groom's hand is raised as he swears a solemn oath.

The dog is a griffin terrier, which was a symbol of loyalty in olden times.

77

Making a collage

collage is an exciting way of making pictures. Instead of using paints or crayons, you cut shapes out of scraps of paper and cloth and small objects and glue them to the paper. It's a bit like doing a jigsaw, only you make the shapes yourself. You can stick the shapes on top of each other as well as next to each other.

Famous artists like Pablo Picasso have made collage pictures. It's great fun to find odd scraps of material and to use your imagination to put them together to make a picture full of exciting colors, shapes and textures. (By *texture*, we mean what things feel like. Pudding has a smooth texture, oatmeal has a knobby texture; cloth has a soft texture, wood has a hard texture, and so on.)

For this portrait Nichola, aged 10, used small squares of colored paper which she had cut from a magazine. The effect is like a Roman mosaic.

Mark, aged 9, used only two kinds of material – wool and nylon – for his collage. But it works very well because he's layered the net to give a nice texture. Tim drew the profile first in pencil.

This picture (by Emma, aged 7) also uses wool for hair, but this time fabric has been used for the face. Look how she's painted on the rosy cheeks. Using paint as well as "bits and pieces" in a collage can give really interesting effects.

All sorts of materials can be used to make a collage. Why not make a "collage collection" of odd scraps from around the house – fabric strips, wrapping paper, pieces of string and wool, buttons, currugated cardboard, pebbles, shells, leaves – in fact, anything that has an interesting color or texture.

You will also need scissors to cut up your collage material, glue, sheets of newspaper to protect the table, and plenty of rags or tissues to mop up any spills.

Get your balance

The human body has two sides to it. When you make a movement on one side, the other side moves in a different direction in order to keep the body balanced. Stand in front of a mirror and shift your weight onto your right foot. Can you see – and feel – how your left leg bends at the knee, your right hip moves up and your left hip moves down? When you draw people, be aware of how the limbs balance each other in different positions. This will help to make your figure drawings more lifelike.

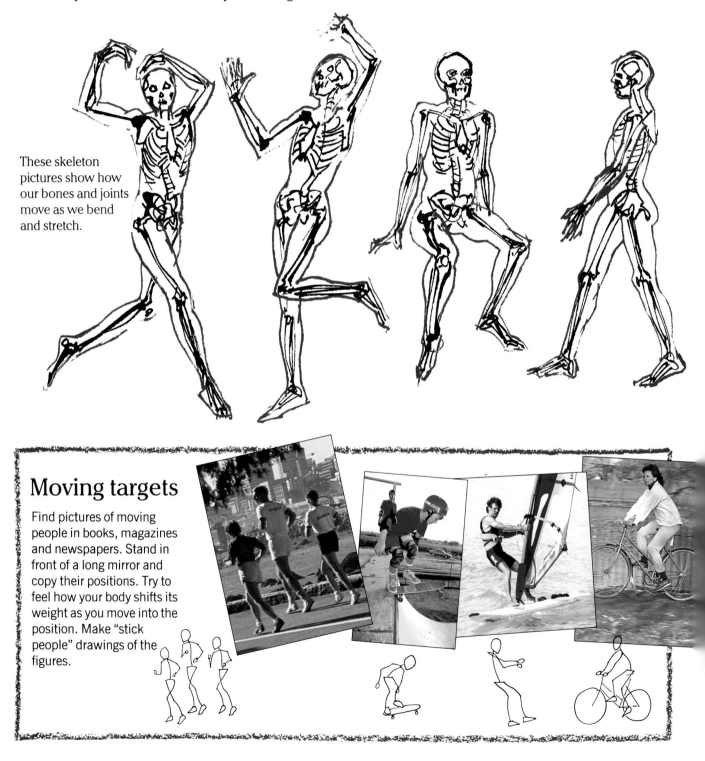

These skeleton pictures show how our bones and joints move as we bend and stretch.

Moving targets

Find pictures of moving people in books, magazines and newspapers. Stand in front of a long mirror and copy their positions. Try to feel how your body shifts its weight as you move into the position. Make "stick people" drawings of the figures.

These sketches show how the body balances itself when it performs different actions. Notice how the body leans away from heavy objects it is pulling or carrying.

Planning your picture

When you paint a picture, think carefully about the people and objects you want to include and where you will place them. Arranging the parts of a picture is called "composition," and a good composition makes a good picture!

Different shapes and sizes add interest and variety to a picture. Overlapping objects and figures will lead the viewer's eye easily from one part to the next. This helps hold the picture together instead of having bits here and there that don't seem to have anything to do with each other. It's best to make some rough sketches first to see which composition works best.

If you want to paint a park scene, for example, think who would bring it to life – you could include a man snoozing in a deckchair, his head covered by a paper, children playing ball, a dog chasing a stick, and a gardener mowing the grass.

Compose your own picture

These figures of boys and girls have been drawn to the scale they would appear if they were positioned in the foreground, the middle ground, or the background of a picture. Trace the figures and use them to make your own compositions. Try making pictures with overlapping figures, and compare them with compositions where the figures have lots of space around them. Two examples have already been done in the boxes.

In this picture all of the figures are standing in a straight line and are all the same size (scale).

In this picture the figures are overlapping. Smaller and larger (middle ground and background) figures have been used, giving the picture a feeling of depth.

Look at the different composition of these pictures. You don't always have to place your model in the center. Experiment by putting him or her at one side of the picture, or by overlapping different people or objects. Using a diagonal composition can help give a sense of movement, as in the picture of the ballet dancers below.

All about scale

Scale means how big or small an object looks when we compare it to another object. For example, a cat is bigger than a mouse, but a cat is much smaller than an elephant!

The odd thing is that when you have two objects of the same size, one close to you and the other far away, the closer object looks much bigger than the one far away. Look at this picture of people sitting in a theater. The two older people in the **foreground** are painted with much bigger heads than the three people behind in the **middle ground**, while the two people farthest away in the **background** have even smaller heads. Painting people different sizes, according to how far away they are, will give your picture the illusion of depth and make it much more interesting to look at.

Finger painting

F inger painting is great fun because you can use your fingers – or even your hand – as a paintbrush! These pictures show just some of the exciting patterns and marks you can make with your fingers, thumbs and hands. See if you can think of some more. Then think about how you can combine different marks to make a finger painting of a figure, or a group of figures. Start by making a few trial prints on scrap paper before working on your picture.

Arty says ...
Finger painting works best if the paint is quite thick. Mix a little wallpaper paste into the paint to thicken it.

For finger painting you will need:

- A sheet of paper
- Newspaper
- Poster paints
- A shallow dish to hold the paint
- Plenty of rags for cleaning your fingers
- Felt-tip pens for adding details to your picture

Make long, squiggly lines by dragging your fingers down the paper.

Make tiny dots and spots by pressing very lightly on the paper.

Press the whole of your index finger into the paint, then press your finger onto the paper to make sausage shapes like these.

Press the edge of your hand into the paint and drag it across the paper.

These shapes are made with the fingertips.

Crowd scenes

Here's a great idea for painting a crowd of people. Mix up two or three dishes of paint in different shades of pink and brown. Dip the tip of your forefinger into the paint and press it onto the paper lots of times to make the face shapes. When the paint is dry, use crayons or felt-tips to add hair and features. Add things like hats, scarves and glasses, too. Here are some places where crowds gather:

- A football game
- A rock concert
- A busy shopping street
- The theater or the movies
- A carnival

These shapes are made from thumbprints.

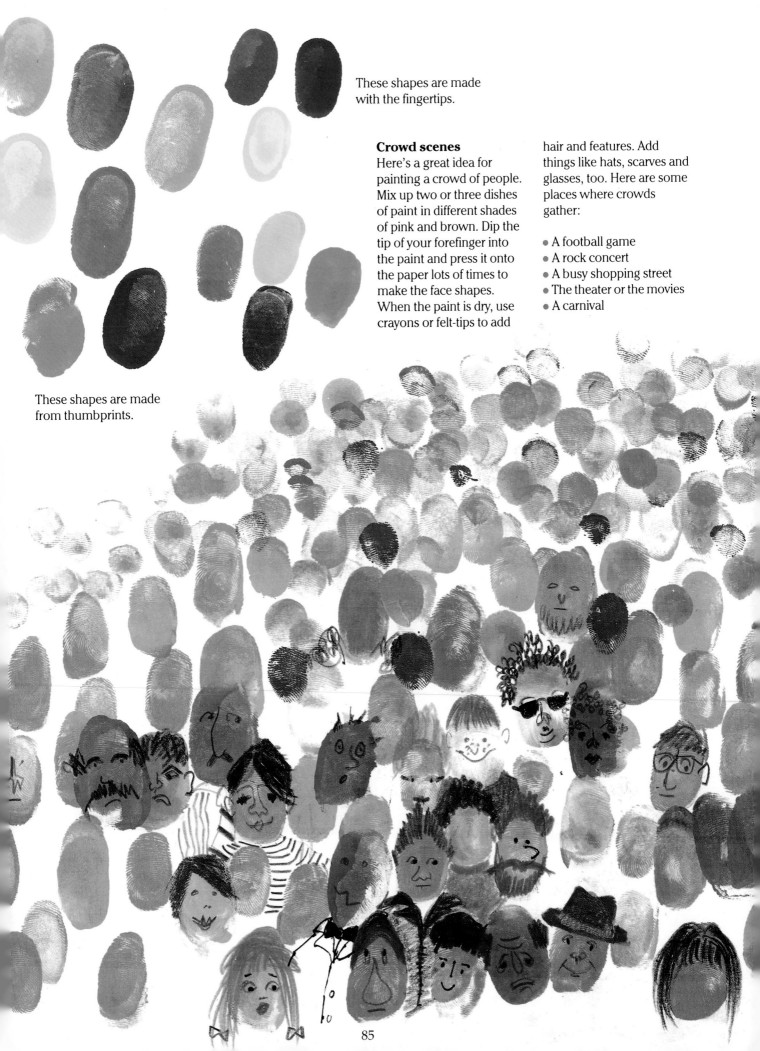

85

Making potato prints

You can make exciting designs and shapes with a potato and some poster paint. Each potato can be cut into two or more pieces to make different designs that can be printed many times. Use potato prints to make repeat patterns for decorating book covers and greeting cards – or use them to make portraits of people or to illustrate a story. When the prints are dry, you can draw more details on them with wax crayons or felt-tip pens.

To make potato prints you will need:

- A raw potato
- Dishes of poster paint
- A sharp knife
- Paper to print onto
- A paint brush
- Crayons or felt-tip pens

Arty says...
Sharp knives can be dangerous, so use them carefully. Hold the potato firmly and keep your fingers away from the knife blade in case it slips. When you cut out the potato shape, cut away from yourself, not toward you. Best of all, get an adult to help you.

Potato-cut cartoons
Invent your own cartoon characters using potato prints. Make simple potato-print face shapes like these. Then, when the paint is dry, use a felt-tip pen to draw amusing features onto the face shapes.

How to make a potato print

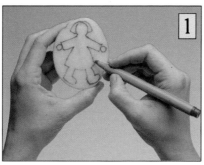

Choose a medium-sized potato and cut it in half. Use a felt-tip pen to draw your design on the cut end of one half of the potato; or draw the shape on some paper, cut it out, place it on the potato and trace around it.

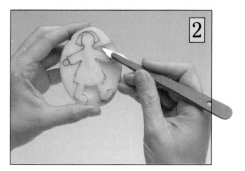

With a sharp knife, cut away the potato around the outside of the shape so that it stands out from the surface.

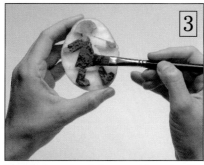

Brush the raised shape with paint. Be careful not to use too much paint, or the finished print will be messy and the colors will run into each other.

Press the potato firmly onto the surface of your paper. You should be able to make two or three prints before applying more paint.

Family and friends

T his painting is called *The Luncheon of the Boating Party*. It was painted in 1881 by Pierre Auguste Renoir, one of the French Impressionist painters. The painting is of a group of people enjoying lunch outdoors on a sunny afternoon. The people in the picture are friends of Renoir. The girl with the dog on the left of the picture is Aline Charigot, who later became Renoir's wife.

The picture has a relaxed, happy feel to it. Can you suggest some ways in which the artist expressed this in his painting? There are some suggestions at the bottom of this page.

Study Renoir's painting and then make your own modern-day version of it. You could paint a scene from a celebration, such as a birthday party or a wedding reception. Or perhaps a family picnic or barbeque. You can paint your picture from real life, from imagination, or using a family snapshot as reference.

The people all have their heads turned toward each other. Some have their arms around each other.

Renoir has used warm, sunny colors in the painting to express a happy mood. There are touches of red and yellow all over the painting.

The expressions on the
faces of the people are
relaxed, and we can tell
they are talking happily.

Copying a work of art

Many of the great artists learned to draw and paint by copying the paintings of artists who had gone before. Copying is a good way to learn, because it is like stepping into an artist's shoes. As you copy, you discover the way the artist used lines, shapes and colors almost without thinking. Then you can use what you have discovered in your own paintings and drawings.

Visit art galleries, or look at pictures of portraits in books. Choose one you really like and make your own copy of it. Try to find out about the artist. What materials and methods did he or she use? Why was the portrait painted? Who was the portrait of?

This is a portrait of the English writer Somerset Maugham. It was painted in 1949 by Graham Sutherland, an English artist. Somerset Maugham loved the Orient and lived there for a long time. There are oriental touches in the painting. Can you spot them? There is a bamboo stool, and you can just see some palm fronds above Mr. Maugham's head. The background is orange, like the robes of a Buddhist monk. Also notice the way Mr. Maugham is sitting and the expression on his face. He looks very aloof and inscrutable, like a wise old man from China. So you see, this portrait is not just a picture of a man. It also tells us something about the man's character and his interests.

Try making a copy of this portrait. The pictures here show copies made by four different children.

Sarah Little, aged 9½

Rhys Wilson, aged 10

Heather Sygrove, aged 11

Finnian Brigham, aged 10

HOW TO DRAW AND PAINT

CARTOONS

and Animation

PAUL JOHNSON

CONTENTS

How to Draw and Paint Cartoons

Papier Mache Project Book

Where to start

NSTEAD OF LOOKING AT OTHER PEOPLE'S cartoons in comic books, magazines, and books, why not try to create some for yourself? Cartoons are fun to draw, and it is a challenge to think of a character, write a good story, and put it all together. This book will show you how!

▲ Greek myths
Many ancient Greeks couldn't read, so stories were told using a series of pictures. This is the same principal as comic strips today.

▲ Basic strip cartoons
Some cartoons are made into a series of pictures called a strip cartoon, which tells a story that is humorous, or serious.

EARLY CARTOONS

When the majority of the world's population was illiterate, stories and happenings were told in pictures. Many churches have stained glass windows showing biblical stories which taught people about religion. Cartoon strips today also tell a story in pictures, although the content is often more humorous than these early examples!

◄ Medieval illustrations
This german medieval picture shows a warrior about to go into battle. Pictures were very detailed and beautifully painted.

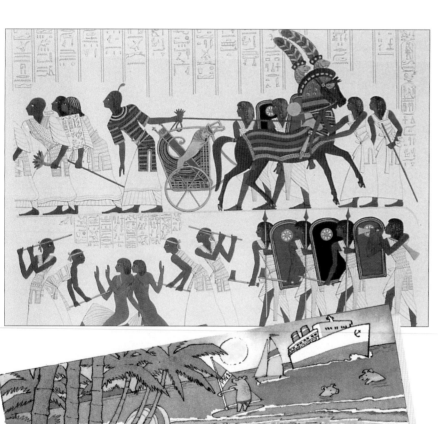

◄ Ancient Egyptian wall paintings
This copy of an ancient Egyptian wall painting shows a famous pharaoh going into battle. There are many wonderful and fantastic legends and events told by Egyptian paintings, especially on tomb walls. Even their writing, called hieroglyphs, was made from pictures and signs.

◄ Comic postcards
Comic postcards have been popular since the nineteenth century. This picture postcard shows a classic cartoon technique of showing animals behaving exactly as though they were human beings.

From pen to paper

A LL YOU NEED AT FIRST IS A PENCIL or pen and plenty of paper, to play around with ideas and develop your characters. Use rough paper to start with, as you might try out several ideas before you are ready to start on the final artwork.

EQUIPMENT

Start drawing in pencil, but not one that is too hard. Try an HB or a B, and lightly sketch out an idea. Then redraw over the lighter lines,

HELP! I'M A GOOD IDEA !!

Use rough paper or a cheap sketchpad in the beginning.

Keep any ideas which look like they could be developed or adapted.

Use a soft pencil, not a hard H pencil, as these are used for fine detail.

▼ Materials

Here are some useful materials. They include inks, watercolors, paints, felt pens, colored crayons, pens, and pastels. You probably will not need all of them, but experiment as much as possible.

▲ Pencils and crayons
Draw and color with pencils and crayons on any paper, but your picture will be neater if you use a paper with a smooth surface. When shading with crayons, try to do it in one direction only and build up the color gradually.

▼ Watercolors and inks
These are wet, so you will need a fairly thick watercolor paper to work on. Remember to do your outline with a waterproof pen or crayon, or else it will run when you start painting.

USING DIFFERENT MEDIUMS

Experiment with different types of medium and colors on various papers to see which you prefer. You may have some artist's materials, such as crayons and colored pens, at home. Or, perhaps you are able to try out others, like chunky felt pens or inks, at school. If you buy any, limit yourself to one or two of each kind, to make sure that you like using them first. There are various types of paper, some have smooth surfaces, and some have rough surfaces which soak in the colors if you use inks or felt pens on them. Keep experimenting until you feel happy with your chosen medium.

Marker pens may bleed (run), on thick paper.

▲ Colored pens and felt pens
Draw your line with a black pen at first, then color in with chunky felt pens. It is best to work on a thin paper called "layout" paper. Chunky felt pens give a good solid, of "flat" color, and try to color in one direction, as with crayons.

► Tracing paper
Tracing paper is very useful for experimenting. You can do one drawing then put it under a sheet of tracing paper, and redraw any changes over it to make sure you like it. You can also flip (turn over) the drawing to see if it looks better the other way round.

Tracing paper with the original sketch underneath.

What style?

YOU COULD TRY TO COPY A STYLE YOU LIKE, BUT IT IS much better to develop your own way of working. That way you will be more original. The more you practice, the quicker your own style will develop.

▲ Simple black line
This line is drawn wobbly on purpose.
Use pen and ink, or a thin black pen.

▲ Chunky felt pens
This simple style is good for drawing cartoons
for very young children.
It is drawn with marker pens.

LINE WORK

You can create many varied styles with the kind of lines you draw. They can be simple or detailed; wobbly or solid. Draw lines with pencil, colored pen, or pen and ink. Use lines for shading, and cross hatching for shading darker areas. The four pictures *(left)* show how different lines and medium make very diverse effects.

▲ Detailed line
Use lines for shading. The cross hatching
(in the kennel) creates even darker areas.

▲ Pen and crayons
This combination of a pen and ink line
with crayons is excellent for cartoons.

SOFTER EFFECTS

Colored crayon will give a soft effect to a drawing.

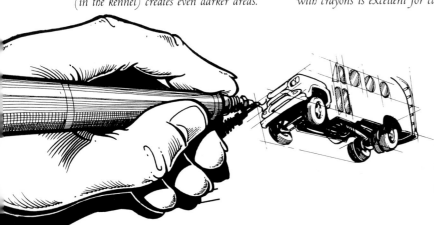

This drawing shows the interesting effects of using a ball point pen.

OTHER STYLES

Study other cartoons to learn about all the different styles and mediums. Borrow ideas that you like, but try drawing them freehand, because it will help you to draw more naturally.

◄ Soft style
Use inks and watercolors for blending different shades of color, and a softer painting. These mediums work best if the paper is damp, so the colors can merge (run) into each other.

◄ Realistic styles
This style is more suited to dramatic stories, rather then funny ones. It is drawn using a fine pen line, cross hatching, and felt pens for the color.

▲ Sun
You may like the way the sun is drawn in one cartoon you see.

▲ Nose
And you may think a nose is funny in another cartoon.

▲ Whole picture
So why not put these two things together in one picture yourself?

What to draw?

THINKS!

Y OU COULD SIT AND STARE AT A BLANK piece of paper waiting for inspiration, but it may never arrive! Instead, look around you, wherever you are – at home, at school, on a bus, or at the zoo. Your cartoon character can be based on a person, an animal, even an inanimate object, or it could be totally from your imagination.

YOU COULD DRAW GOLDFISH, CATS, HAMSTERS, RABBITS, EVEN STICK INSECTS!!

BABIES

Some people are naturally funny. Babies are great to draw. Their big heads on little bodies already make them look like a cartoon. Practice drawing them both in real life and from a photograph, and in various positions – sitting, crawling, or tottering about.

I HOPE I GET PAID FOR POSING!

HMMM..... NOT BAD FOR A BEGINNER!

PETS

Pets make very good cartoon characters, and they will not complain about the likeness! Try sketching them from life, but if they keep moving or it is too difficult, draw them from photographs or magazines.

FAMILIES

Draw the people in your family doing everyday things, such as cooking or watching television. Before long, you could have drawn a cartoon family.

MUM

DAD

SISTER

▲ Photographic reference
Use photographs you have of your family, friends, and pets to study different positions, faces, expressions, and characteristics.

▲ Studying people
Study strangers as well as friends. Each person has a unique characteristic or manner which can be turned into part of a cartoon.

RESEARCH

It is very useful if you can always carry a sketchpad with you in case you see a face or a character that could be adapted into a cartoon. You will find things that can be part of your cartoon in everyday life, or if you go on a special trip. The zoo is a great place to study and draw a wide range of animals, which you would normally only see in books or on the television.

▼ Media
Look carefully at people and creatures on the television, and keep newspaper cuttings in a scrapbook of anything interesting.

▲ Studying animals
At the zoo you can study how the animals look, as well as the way they move, wash, and eat.

Body forms

IN MOST CARTOONS ONE OR TWO FEATURES of the body are usually exaggerated. This creates the humor of the drawing. If you learn to draw normal human bodies first, you can then experiment with cartoon versions – perhaps drawing very fat, thin, tall, or short bodies.

HOW TO DRAW

A good basic way to start drawing people is to make a simple figure first, and gradually add on more detailed features and clothes to give your person a unique character.

◀ Stick figures
You can start by drawing a stick figure, and then drawing round it to give it clothes, hands, and feet. Also, try drawing it in different positions such as walking or sitting. Keep it simple.

◀ Ovals and circles
Another way is to draw the body as a series of ovals and circles. Where the ovals join are the joints of the body. You can then experiment with fatter or thinner ovals to create different body shapes and characteristics.

LOOKING AT PEOPLE

Look carefully at your subject, and just draw what you see. It does not matter if it's not a masterpiece, or if you get some things wrong. Mistakes can sometimes be useful or funny. It is best to draw from life, but if you need a difficult position you can use photographs. But try to avoid tracing the body, as this will not help you to understand its shape.

◄ From photo to sketchpad
It can be useful to look at a photograph to study a person's dominant characteristics closely. Use these to create a cartoon figure in your sketchpad.

PEOPLE SHAPES

Heads stay almost the same size, but the height of the body changes with age. Cartoon characters often have small bodies and big heads as the face is very important.

▼ Cross section
Draw a whole age range of people from a baby to an old person. This is a good way to examine how the body changes with age.

Big head!

THE HEAD IS THE MOST IMPORTANT feature on a cartoon person, so it is worth learning how to draw it well. Once you have mastered the basic shape, it is easy to add on different features, such as hairstyles, beards, and glasses. You can then try drawing a side- or back-view of a head.

▲ Shapes
A real head is not round like a football, but slightly oval in shape.

HEADS AND NECKS

Give a thin person a neck, and a slightly longer oval shaped head. But a fat head sits right on the shoulders, and is a rounder and fatter oval shape. Experiment with the shape of the head until you are happy with it, as it will be such an important feature in your cartoon.

► Proportions
This is a good way to draw a correct head. The eyes go just above the centerline.

► Adding features
This is the correct place to put in the nose and mouth.

► Hair
Add the eyebrows, eyelashes, and the hair last. The hair is also an important feature.

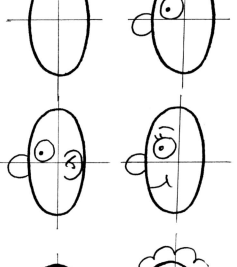

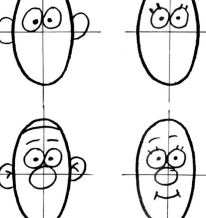

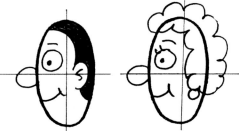

Some people have very big chins on long, thin faces.

Reverse the long, thin face to create the opposite effect.

Some heads are long and thin but egg shaped.

Beards and mustaches can be added to your basic head shape.

ADDING FEATURES

You can add on extra features to your basic head and face. Everything goes toward creating expression and character. Think about different hairstyles, noses, mouths, and eyes. Glasses can be used with different characters, from old people, to fierce teachers, to mad scientists.

Beards can be big and bushy, drawn with an outline and colored in. Mustaches can be a few lines, or large and curly.

HAIRSTYLES

Hair can be drawn as a scribble, a solid black line, or as an outline to be filled in with color. Useful tips are that babies have very little hair, and old men tend to go bald.

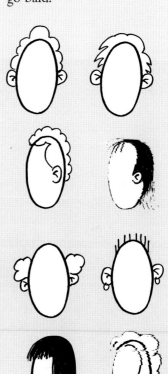

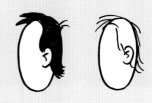

BASIC DETAILS

Cartoon eyes, noses, and mouths are usually big to allow more room for exaggerated expression. Eyes can be sleepy, weepy, or scared, and mouths can be happy, sad, or surprised.

Cartoon creatures

IF YOU WANT TO MAKE A CARTOON creature, first practice how to draw the real thing. This will help you to understand its individual characteristics. Once you know an animal well, it is much easier to play around with a sketch of it and work out what you would like to emphasize. Some animals are naturally funny, and baby animals are especially good if you want a cute character.

WHICH ANIMAL TO CHOOSE?

You can choose any animal you like, and they need not be real. Dinosaurs are fun to draw, because they are extinct you can be very imaginative! This spread looks at all the different features of animals that you can put in your cartoon.

you're shocking!

Some animals are furry. It is a good technique to exaggerate this.

Huge animals make excellent cartoon subjects.

Some creatures are scaly and spikey, which can make them fierce or funny.

And so do tiny ones. You can use insects as well as animals.

▲ Funny animals
Some animals are naturally funny. Here are a few examples — ostriches, pigs, tree frogs, ardvaarks, crocodiles, and toucans. Just pick the feature you think is the funniest and really exaggerate it in your drawing. If an animal is not odd looking, then you might have to emphasize more than one characteristic.

RESEARCH

Try to avoid animals which have been made into cartoons many times, unless you can think of a new way to draw them. There are plenty of ways of finding amusing or interesting animals. The zoo will have unusual ones, and parks or farms will have many animals that you can sketch.

USING PICTURES

You can always just copy animals and ideas from books, magazines and the television. Or, even look at paintings in art galleries.

ANIMAL FEATURES

Particular animals will have their own obvious features, and it is these you need to study well so you can exaggerate them in your cartoon. Here are some obvious examples, but keep an eye out all the time for new and funny ideas.

Give dogs wet noses, wagging tails, and floppy or pricked up ears.

Pigs need big snouts, curly tails and ears that flop about.

This duck has an extra large beak.

▶ Feet

It is easy to forget the importance of feet, but they are funny and varied, and can be full of character. Birds and monsters have scaly skin and sharp claws; ducks have webbed feet; and elephants have enormous toenails!

Animal antics

Y OU CAN CHOOSE JUST ONE CREATURE to make into a cartoon, but it would get a bit lonely! So add a friend, or even an enemy. Or maybe you could create a whole cartoon jungle, a woodland scene, or an undersea world. You can also use your imagination to make your own animals up.

WHAT TO CHANGE?

It is up to you how much you change an animal into a cartoon. Do you make four legged animals stand up and walk? Do you give them clothes to wear, or alter their natural colors? The only rule is to take care that their special features, such as a tiger's stripes or a rabbit's ears, remain recognizable.

1 *One way to draw a cartoon creature is to sketch out a rough, simple shape first of all.*

2 *Add the animal's special, main features. Dogs need predominant noses, eyes and ears, and a tail to wag.*

3 *Make your animal happy with a big smile, like this dog, or sad with a downturned mouth.*

4 *Now fill in the details to make your cartoon character complete. This dog has a shiny, wet nose, bright eyes, and a panting tongue.*

Draw a real hare first. Keep its big ears, teeth, and tail as you change it.

It stands up and its paws become hands.

Dress it as you want, but keep its big ears and buck teeth.

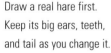

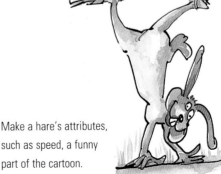

Make a hare's attributes, such as speed, a funny part of the cartoon.

▲ Manic panic
A huge grin, big round eyes, and copious amounts of wild fur make this cat look manic, even though its shape is very basic and can be drawn easily.

ANIMAL CHARACTERISTICS

As you work think about the sort of character you want your creature to have. Is it to be clever, or maybe a bit dumb? Will it have a special attribute, such as speed or strength? The face is an important place to create character, and some creatures already look naturally wicked, clever or dumb. But there are lots of things you can do. Sometimes you will need to keep its real color to help keep its identity – a bat must be black to be spooky. With most four-legged creatures, it's possible to make them stand on their hind legs, and use their front paws as hands. And with birds, you can adapt the feathers on the wings to look like arms and hands, or get rid of the wings altogether and draw arms instead. Think about whether it wears clothes, and if so, what kind?

▶ Dumb or bright?
This cartoon dog is a blood hound. This type of dog looks dumb anyway, but its features have been exaggerated to give it slow, sleepy eyes and a lumbering shape. In contrast, the bird is quick-witted, and quick-limbed. Its glasses and book are clear, recognizable reflections of a clever character.

▶ Wild and wicked
Vultures are usually depicted as wicked and sly in cartoons. Note the angry eyes and pointing finger. The crocodile's big teeth are its main feature.

Anything goes

CARTOONS ARE ABLE TO BREATHE LIFE into anything. Unlike photographs or live action movies, any object will come to life given a face, a pair of hands, and a pair of legs. The face is where you can show its personality most easily, as a mouth or eyes will make any object happy or sad, tired or worried.

▼ Magic pencils!
With your pencil and some imagination you can magic anything into life!

BRING IT TO LIFE

For inspiration on which objects to bring to life look all around you – in your bedroom, kitchen, school, or yard. Types of plants make good cartoons, especially vegetables. You could turn your house into a character, with windows for eyes and a door for the mouth, and create a cartoon family to live in it.

Think how a
saucepan would
feel if it were alive.

Would a tea cup feel
proud or annoyed to be
filled with hot tea?

Do pedal bikes secretly
yearn to be the speed
kings of the road?

As if by magic!

ONCE YOU HAVE AN IDEA DRAW lots of doodles on rough paper. Try to emphasize one particular feature of your object. If you bring a brick to life, make it look heavy; if you choose a balloon, it must look light. Try shapes that are fairly simple to draw, because the fewer the unimportant details the better.

CARS

Cars are good to draw because there are so many types and you can have fun with their personalities. Draw friendly, little cars with rounded lines and a smiling bumper; or fast, aggressive cars with a long radiator for a mouth and wicked eyes instead of the headlights.

Other ideas
Trains, planes, boats, and tankers are also popular. Think up something to make your character different, such as a boat that doesn't like water, or an airplane that is scared of heights.

A Family of Objects

Perhaps you may decide to have a number of objects all living in one place, such as cups and saucers, teapots, and knives and forks whose home is the kitchen. Think what their personalities may be – is the china delicate, are the pots and pans tough? Do they all like each other, or are there certain characters who are always arguing or sulking with each other?

◄ **Personalize objects**
Cutlery is easy to give a personality to, as they already have "bodies" and "hairstyles." Just add a face, and maybe arms and legs, and they come alive.

► **Main characters**
You could have a main object character, such as "Teapot Tim," or "Sally Sugar." Learn to draw it well from all different angles. Draw it so often that it becomes a friend. It is common in cartoons to have an object, which although secondary to an animate character, is still the leader of the inanimate object gang.

Fantasy characters

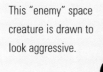 IF YOU HAVE A VIVID IMAGINATION your cartoon character can come entirely from your mind. Fantasy subjects are ideal for cartoons and animation. You can escape from the real world and invent what you like – as long as you can draw it! Fantasy creatures can live in a completely made-up world, in outer space, or even inside the human body.

▲ Wonderman!
This realistic, superhero style is good for dramatic action-packed stories.

STRANGE SHAPES

Fantastic fantasy characters and monsters can be humorous or serious. Space creatures, for instance, can be funny shapes and colors, or hard and menacing with angular lines and metallic colors.

▲ Dinosaurs
Dinosaurs are a good basis from which to draw imaginative ones. You can mix up various types to create your own.

This "enemy" space creature is drawn to look aggressive.

Ghosts are soft and loose and can be any shape you want.

Robots are the opposite to ghosts, with strong colors and clear lines.

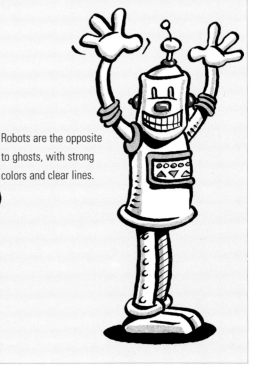

Silhouettes

Use black ink to paint silhouettes, which are good for spooky ghosts, shadows, and bats.

Mix animals to create a fantasy friend, or foe.

Sharp teeth, and fierce eyes make this silly creature scary.

Characters Need Stories

There are no limits to what you can draw, but whether it is funny or action-packed, you still need a good storyline. You could invent the most wonderful fantasy characters ever seen, but they are lifeless until there is a plot. So as well as what they look like, think about what they will do, and how they will do it.

1 *Your super-character will begin life brimming with action and enthusiasm.*

2 *But with no plot or enemies to conquer, his powers will soon start to fade away.*

3 *So now is the time to create a story for your character — or he will soon fall fast asleep.*

Fairytale foes

THE CLASSIC CARTOON SCENARIO involves a battle between two different characters. They can be good or evil, strong, or weak, clever or stupid. Many cartoon characters have been inspired by ancient myths, fairytales, and legends. There are innocent types such as pixies, elves, and gnomes; and more sinister ones such as ghosts, vampires, witches, and wizards.

Scientists are good or evil – fighting to either save or destroy the world.

IMAGINATION

It is easy to show who is good, and who is bad. Draw evil characters with dark colors, black clothes, downturned mouths, and pointed noses. Good characters can be drawn with soft lines, and pale or bright colors. Some characters can be good or bad, such as skeletons or ghosts, depending on their facial expressions. But the good guys will always need an enemy with whom to fight, and vice versa.

Vampires wear black, with blood-stained fangs, and often have a bat nearby.

Fairies are usually good, but also mischievous.

MYTHICAL FIGURES

You will find many good ideas in books on myths and legends that are full of strange creatures, such as centaurs, mermaids, and giants. Many myths have monsters which are half-animal, half-human, especially the Greek Myths. You can make up your own strange and wonderful combinations.

▲ Mermaids
Although mermaids are half-human, half-creature, they are rarely shown as monstrous, but rather attractive and elegant.

▲ Witches
Draw wicked witches with pointed noses and chins, tall hats, and dark clothes. They are often accompanied by a black cat called a "familiar."

► Giants
Giants are a popular fairytale figure, so you can find lots of visual references for them. This drawing uses perspective to make the giant look very tall (see pp. 50-51). Giants can be gentle or blood-thirsty.

Giving it life

THINK ABOUT HOW THE CHARACTER WILL ACT, AS IF IT WERE A real person. What will make it different or special? Write a list of things it can or can't do, and start to draw pictures of it from different angles. In this way you will build up a character sheet that you can refer to while you draw.

CREATING YOUR CHARACTER

Your character sheet could look something like this (below). Use it to remind you of the way your character looks and acts, otherwise you can discover that it looks different at the end of your cartoon strip than at the start. Give your character a catchy name.

► Hands

Hands can express a lot about your cartoon character, and even cartoon hands need plenty of drawing practice. If your character is a superhero, he will need realistic hands, but others can be very simple. Often cartoonists draw hands with just a thumb and three fingers.

► Feet

Feet and footwear are as important a part of human cartoon characters as animal ones. Barefeet can be very varied, and are often funny. Feet also show the way a person walks, runs, or stands. And different types of shoes indicate a great deal about the character's age, taste, and profession.

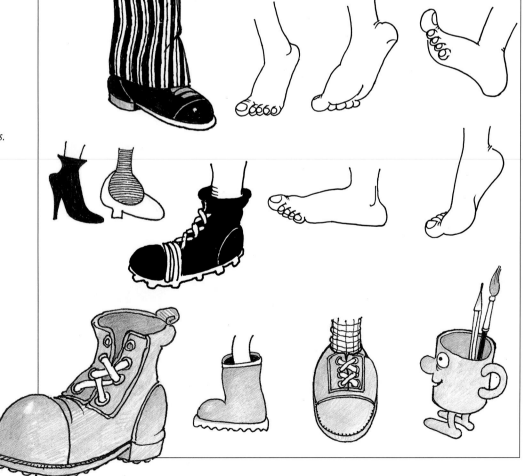

Expressive faces

YOUR CARTOON FACE NEEDS TO BE able to show the whole range of human emotions. But you must be able to do this with the minimum of drawing, so that the particular emotion you want to convey is really obvious. You will notice that most expressions are shown with the mouth and eyes.

Faces show the whole spectrum of human feelings.

◄ Different styles
Different styles make different characters. The three boxes (below) show, firstly, a really simple cartoon style, suitable for a short joke; the next shows a more detailed character, which you could develop farther; the last realistic style is good for an action comic strip with a serious, dramatic content. In the end, you should decide what style and level you feel confident with, and work from there.

 **+**  **+**  **=**

1 *Experiment with a face by drawing a blank, or nearly blank, head to start.*

2 *Add on different hairstyles drawn on tracing paper placed over the original.*

3 *Try drawing a mustache, or any other feature, on another sheet of tracing paper.*

4 *Complete the picture with a beard on a third tracing paper layer.*

FACIAL FEATURES

All human beings have the same basic features, so their individuality depends on how you draw them. There are standard ways of drawing different emotions. Scared people's hair stands on end; surprise is shown by raised eyebrows, and sleepy people have half-closed eyes. Make faces at yourself in the mirrror to study different expressions.

▼ Noses
Cartoon noses are generally exaggerated to make the face funnier. They can be made longer, bigger, or into a button shape for babies.

▼ Hair
Many well-known cartoon characters have distinctive hairstyles. Hair can make your character look scruffy, glamorous, young, or old.

▼ Eyes
Eyes can be simple black dots; more expressive eyes are dots in white circles, or semi-circles, with eyebrows.

▼ Mouths
The simplest mouth is just a line and a solid black shape when it opens. A mouth can have teeth, shown as a block or as individual teeth.

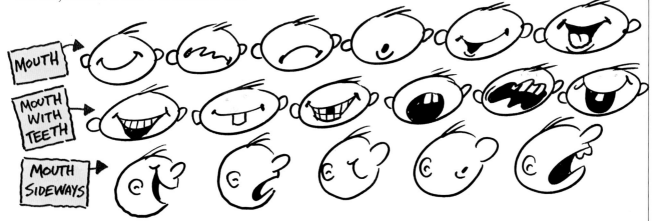

On the move

NOW YOU HAVE CREATED your ideal character, and given it a name and an identity, you need to make it have adventures, or get into tricky situations. And for this you need to make it move.

▲ Oops!
Getting flattened by a heavy weight and becoming paper-thin is a classic cartoon joke.

MOVEMENT

When someone walks they have one or both feet on the ground. But when they run draw both feet off the ground to help give the impression of speed.

Your character can stroll along (left), or really whizz along (below).

IT'S FISH LADY!

▲ Fish lady!
Your character can grow an extra feature, such as wings or fins to enable it to swim or fly as part of the story.

DANGER HIGH CLIFF

▲ Watch out!
Cartoon characters "tread water" in mid-air before they fall off cliffs. Draw speed marks to show fast movement.

BODY BUILDING KIT

10 TONS

WHAT CAN YOUR CHARACTER DO?

The wonderful thing about cartoons is that you can make your character do absolutely anything, as long as you are able to draw it!

Much cartoon humor is "slapstick" and involves such things as cliffs, danger signs, or ten-ton weights. Violence has always been an element in cartoons. It is not the real world, so characters get squashed, dropped, or blown up and still survive.

YOUR CARTOON CHARACTER CAN DO ANYTHING!

Your character can fly to outerspace, and all sorts of other exciting and dangerous acts!

▶ Action
Your character can go anywhere, even catch a rocket to the moon. Since it is not the real world, anything is believable.

Your character can grow tiny or bigger than the world itself.

A huge bump on the head is a classic bit of "slapstick" humor.

Human oddballs

LOOK AROUND YOU AT THE ENDLESS variety of people. They are all possible subjects! Your comic strip could become really boring if all the people in it looked the same, so here are a selection of other types who could also feature.

Good little children have neat clothes and hair.

Naughty kids have scruffy clothes and hair, and a wicked grin!

CHILDREN

All your cartoon children should have different personalities. Some may never do anything wrong, and be little angels. And others may be just the opposite, always getting into trouble, playing practical jokes and pranks. Maybe they are smart, or very streetwise?

Babies have big heads, little wobbly bodies, and huge mouths!

◀ Foreigners
Here are some stereotypes of different races. They may be useful as "extras" in your cartoons, or you can develop them farther if you want.

HISTORY

You can also do an historical cartoon strip. Lots of characters from history are fun to draw, and their costumes make them instantly recognizable. Try Vikings, Romans, cavemen, or Native Americans, for instance.

▼ Comic references
Look through comic books and newspapers to find lots of stereotypes of different ages, characters, and people's dress-sense. Do not copy them exactly, but use them to give you ideas for extra people, like parents or relatives, in your cartoon.

Crazy work

SOME OF THE CHARACTERS IN YOUR cartoon strip could have jobs. The storyline could then include things to do with going to work or problems involved in their jobs. Perhaps a chef who can't cook, or a scientist whose experiments never work or have odd results. The character can be bungling or brilliant at the job – but bungling is funnier!

CARTOON JOBS

Schoolteachers often feature in cartoons. You could base one on a teacher that you know – but don't be too unkind! The picture (below) shows good ideas on what to include when you draw a teacher.

▼ Other professions
Some jobs are naturally funny, or outrageous, like this pop star. You could give your character a job that you would really love to have, or one that you think would be really boring – your character could think so too!

128

ACCESSORIES

Give your character items to carry or wear which help make the job really obvious.

Soldiers should look <u>unlike</u> the ideal recruit.

▶ Attention!
Real soldiers are supposed to be fit and alert, so to create funny ones make them look bored and unfit. Give them big boots and oversized helmets which almost cover their eyes.

THE ARTS

Artists are easy to draw as they wear paint smeared smocks and berets, and will always have a palette and paint brush in their hands.

TRANSFORMATION

The character could be an ordinary working person by day, but at night, an amazing transformation takes place to create someone larger than life!

1 *To make a strong contrast your ordinary person must be very normal, or boring and weak looking. You could use dull colors to emphasize this point.*

2 *You need a special way in which the transformation takes place. Maybe while running, spinning around, or in a phone box — anywhere you want!*

3 *The superhero, or heroine, needs to look very strong and dynamic. Perhaps with a brightly colored special outfit, and bulging muscles to help their battle against evil.*

Cool creatures

REAL ANIMALS DON'T SHOW FACIAL expressions in the same way that humans do. You can't tell if a bird or frog is happy or sad by its face. But once animals become cartoon characters they need to be able to show all the same emotions as humans, otherwise they will have no personality.

◀ Ducks
A real duck bill is very rigid, but a cartoon one is flexible to show different expressions.

▼ Animal babies
Animal babies are good for showing really cute, or slightly pathetic, emotions.
These puppy dogs (below) show how to draw an animal changing from happy to unsure, to exhausted and unhappy. Note the steadily drooping tails and ears, and the drops of sweat (or tears) on the last puppy.

EXPRESSIONS

A cartoon creature's feelings – just like a cartoon human's – are centered in the mouth (or beak), and the eyes. So these particular features should be drawn and made to move in an exaggerated way.

For example, cartoon frogs could have very wide mouths which are long and thin when shut, but can open to talk, or laugh, just like a human being, and you can give them a human-looking tongue. Bears have button eyes, and smiling mouths (right), which make them look friendly, but just add teeth and they become fierce. Look at the other ideas on these pages for good ways to draw expressive faces on a variety of creatures.

◀ Monkeys
Monkeys have very wide mouths which go right across their faces. Their mouths can stretch and twist into all sorts of strange expressions. Their eyes are positioned high up on their heads.

◀ Dogs
Dogs can have very expressive ears as well as faces. A cartoon dog will smile and prick up its ears when it is happy. But when it is sad its mouth and ears will droop right down. Draw dots instead of whiskers.

▼ Cats
Draw cats' emotions in the same way as dogs, but note that they also have big whiskers that reflect a feline's mood.

▼ Insects
Greatly exaggerate insects' eyes and mouths, so that they have enough room to have expressions like any other creature.

Wiggles and waddles

ANIMALS MOVE IN SUCH A VARIETY of ways, all of them very different from humans. You may have decided to make your animal character walk on two legs, but even then creatures walk differently – a penguin waddles, a snake slithers, and a kangaroo hops.

HOW DIFFERENT CREATURES MOVE

The way a creature is drawn moving can add a great deal to its character – and understanding this movement will help when it comes to animation later on in the book. Some creatures, such as snakes or fish, can't walk anyway – or can they? On the other hand you may have created a pig that flies or an elephant that rides a scooter!

▼ Jumping
Frogs and kangaroos jump very high, but in different ways. Frogs stretch right out, but kangaroos bounce up and down.

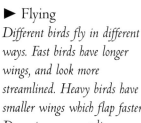
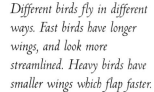

► Flying
Different birds fly in different ways. Fast birds have longer wings, and look more streamlined. Heavy birds have smaller wings which flap faster. Draw in movement lines.

CHARACTERISTIC MOVEMENT

Animals running on all fours stretch out their legs,
then pull them all in together (except horses that use
alternate legs). Four-legged animals running on two
legs use their front limbs as arms. Birds with long legs
walk slowly and pick their feet up, while chickens and
ducks scrape and waddle.

▶ Monkeys
Monkeys swing hanging from one arm or their tail.
Draw their arms much longer than their legs.

◀ Mice
Follow the rule that when a mouse runs on
either four or two legs, all their legs are off
the ground. If they are on their hind legs,
use their front legs as arms in a human
running position.

◀ Penguins
Penguins cannot fly, so they have small
wings but big feet. They waddle and slip
over on the ice, which can look very funny.

◀ Fish
Fish bend their tails to swim. Or you can
make one walk with tail fins as feet.

EEK!

BIG BRICK WALL.

Basic backgrounds

ONCE YOU'VE DESIGNED THEM, YOUR characters will need scenes to be in, whether it's a real or a fantasy world. The scene, or background, can help in all sorts of ways. It makes the cartoon more interesting, and shows if it's set in contemporary or historical time, and where the action is taking place — in a city, the country, or outer-space.

SCENERY

As you plan a scene, think about whether it is indoor or outdoor, and how your character will be placed in it — in the foreground or a speck?

◄ Scenery behind?
Your character is <u>in</u> the scene, so the scenery need not always be behind the character.

◄ Detail
An indoor scene could have just a door and a window, but most rooms have all sorts of things in them.

BASIC BACKGROUNDS

Think of the different places you have been to, maybe on vacation, or even scenes you have seen in magazines or on television. But keep the scene fairly simple, so that it is really obvious what kind of background view it is.

▼ A River
A simple cartoon river is painted blue with paler colored ripples on it.

▼ A Beach
Keep the sea simple, and don't do too many waves. The sand should be a speckled yellow.

SCENERY RESEARCH

When you plan a general background scene think of where your characters will be positioned in it. Don't make the scene so cluttered that there is no space for them. And you can try to make the actual scenery humorous or dramatic to suit the story.

In a space scene do the sky a dark color, and the rest in unusual colors.

Position your characters carefully in the scenery.

▼ A Park

Draw a park bench with railings, simple trees, and some pigeons.

▼ A Staircase

Indoor views are drawn with fairly straight lines.

▼ A Rough Sea

Draw sharp pointed waves. If you add a boat, do it at a dramatic sharp tilt.

Perspective is easy!

EVEN THOUGH YOUR DRAWING IS A flat picture on flat paper, you can create an illusion of depth and distance by using perspective. This will enable you to draw objects from any angle.

▼ Distance
Perspective is the way to show distance in your drawings. To understand perspective, look down a highway or railroad. As the lines of the railroad (below) or highway (right) go farther away from you, they seem to get smaller until they disappear at a "vanishing point."

The near cactus looks bigger than the distant one.

The distant sleepers look smaller.

▲ Vanishing point
The girl in the picture (above) is pointing to the "vanishing point" where the road disappears on the horizon level.

PERSPECTIVE ANYWHERE

Perspective works in any direction that you look. So, if you look up, near things are big and far things are small, and it will be the same if you look down.

The angle of perspective you use may influence the shape of the frame (see pp. 64-65) you create for your cartoon. You can create really dramatic scenes if you use perspective in an interesting way, but even using it a little will make your picture look less flat.

Look down a tall building. The cars are tiny, and the building narrows toward the sidewalk.

Look up a tall building and the top looks narrower, and the clouds and airplanes are small.

Dramatic shots

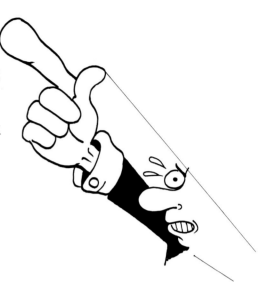

ONCE YOU GET THE HANG OF SIMPLE perspective you can try out some really unusual angles. They may not look right at first, but keep practicing. Sometimes they can really add to the excitement of a cartoon strip.

CHARACTER PERSPECTIVE

Perspective not only works on backgrounds, but can also be used to draw the characters themselves. It's a little harder as there are less straight lines, but it can create dynamic action pictures. Perspective can be useful to show the difference between large and small characters in the same cartoon frame (left and below).

The dinosaur is drawn in perspective. Its great height is shown by the difference in size between its feet and head. Perspective emphasizes the fact that the dinosauris standing behind the child in the foreground.

◄ Bird's eye view

Imagine that a bird is looking down on the flying boy. It would see a person with a big head, and a body that narrows down to small feet. The effect is even more pronounced by the huge hand right in the foreground of the picture, and the relatively small buildings down below.

◄ Worm's eye view

In contrast, imagine that a worm is just out of sight at the bottom of the picture and is looking up at the boy. It would see enormous feet, and a body narrowing to a small head. Also note that the trees get narrower toward the sky. This all helps to create a very dramatic picture in which character perspective and background perspective work well together.

Moody scenes

MAKING A STRIP CARTOON IS LIKE making a movie. You need a good storyline, a superstar (your character), the right setting (your backgrounds), different camera angles (the perspective), and finally the lighting and dramatic effects department to enhance the atmosphere!

DAY SCENES

To create different atmospheres in day scenes you can draw or paint different types of skies.

These suns range from very hot (left), to a setting sun (middle), to a bright day sun (right).

NIGHT SCENES

Night scenes help to show the passage of time, and to create a spooky atmosphere. Show warm-colored lights shining from a dark building, and the moon and stars.

▼ Calm, sunny day
This is shown by blue skies and clouds that look like cotton wool balls.

▼ Cloudy
The sky is filling up with less friendly looking clouds.

▲ Storms approaching
Storm clouds are large, dark, and ominous and take up most the of sky.

▲ Sunsets and sunrises
The sun is low on the horizon, and the sky is pink and orange.

WEATHER

Weather can change a scene dramatically, and it is quite easy to draw. Try snow or rain (below) or flashes of lightning.

SHADOWS

Putting shadows in pictures adds to the realism. Although real shadows are blue/black in tone, cartoon ones are effective as solid black.

A sun high in the sky makes short shadows.

A sun low in the sky makes long shadows.

Forefront light puts the background in shadow.

Background light puts the forefront in shadow.

ALTERNATIVE METHODS

Scary scenes will create the right kind of atmosphere if your character is frightened – like this man below!

Get in shape!

YOU HAVE NOW DESIGNED your cartoon characters and worked out how to do backgrounds and special effects. Your next step is to put them together to make a series of interesting and clever scenes. Experiment with different ways until you find the most effective.

▲ Dream worlds
Use a wiggly frame to create a dream bubble shape. This makes it obvious that the character is dreaming he is flying, rather than actually flying.

◄ Split frames
This technique is also used on the television or in the movies, at it is a very clear way to show two people in different places talking to each other on the telephone.

▲ Through the keyhole
Frame a character or an object as though someone is looking through a keyhole. A pair of binoculars is also very effective.

◄ Caught in the act
Highlighting a character in a shaft of light, such as torchlight, or under a street lamp, will create a dramatic composition.

SPECIAL EFFECTS

This spread looks at a variety of ways to make your pictures have a genuine impact. One way is by putting different frames round your pictures (see pp. 64-65); another method is to vary the size and shape of images within the frame.

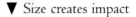

▼ Size creates impact
Using silhouettes against a huge sun or moon will liven up potentially uninteresting scenes. Also, simple scenes like these (below) can make an effective gap between two busy scenes.

◄ Zoom in and out
Just as a movie camera zooms in and out on different scenes, so you can by changing the space filled by your character.

◄ Change the shape
You can have wide scenes (or tall ones). Wide scenes are great for vast, lonely expanses like seas or deserts.

Titles and type

It is best to give a strip cartoon a title, especially if you intend to do more than one. It's a good idea to have the name of your main character in the title, or just have its name as the title, so it's easily remembered. "Terry Dactyl" sounds more catchy than, "The Adventures of Terry Dactyl," and it is a lot less hard work to hand letter each time.

Title Lettering

Title lettering is very important as it will be the first thing that people look at in the cartoon strip. You can create a variety of styles, which match the content of the cartoon. For funny cartoons, don't make your lettering look too serious, and hand draw them, rather than use a ruler. If your cartoon is full of action and adventure, make your lettering look dramatic; if your character wears a stripy shirt, make your title stripy too.

◄ Type styles
These letters show a wild west, a stone age, a horror story, and a futuristic style. Or you could do letters shaped like bubbles, or decorated with patterns, or chunky with drop shadows.

▼ Logos
The title lettering can incorporate the main character, and this becomes a "logo." Put this at the start of your cartoon.

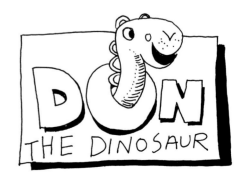

BUT I DISTINCTLY HEARD YOU SAY 'WAITER'!

◄ Simple captions
For simple, single cartoons you can just have the "punchline," as a caption rather than combining the text and the picture.

This style is very simple and effective, and it is often used in cartoons in newspapers.

◄ Expressive words
You can use letters to express feelings, either emotional or physical. This picture shows, in a humorous fashion, the confusion of the detective, the anger of the person on the other end of the telephone, and the mood of the girl — all without any proper words.

WORDS OR NOT ?

Some cartoons are so obvious that they don't need any captions or type, especially the humorous black and white type; they may not even need a title. This allows them to be understood by people from any country.

▼ Pictures that tell a story
This picture tells the story with no words at all. You can do a whole strip without words, but the pictures must be clear and simple.

Crash, bang! Ouch!

THERE ARE MANY DIFFERENT ways to add humorous effects to your pictures. Some are a means of showing sound, while others perhaps indicate movement, show pain, or special lighting effects. You may be able to invent some of your own, and they all help to make the cartoon strip look more visual and fun. Try to imagine new sound effects and then right them down – Kerplunk!

PICTORIAL SOUND EFFECTS

Some sound effects do not need words to be clear. If someone is hit on the head they will see stars, and their head will "spin" around and around (see above). Explosions are fun to draw with clouds of smoke, whirls, and exclamation marks. A bright idea is usually shown by a light bulb above the head.

◀▼ **Action lines**
These lines show objects and characters performing an action. Make the lines suit the picture: this bell (see below) has wavy "sound" lines, and the spilt drink (see left) looks like drops of liquid.

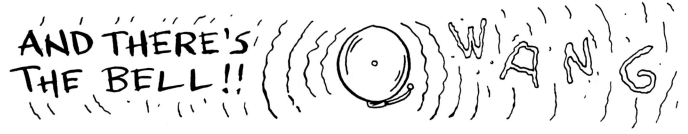

AND THERE'S THE BELL!!

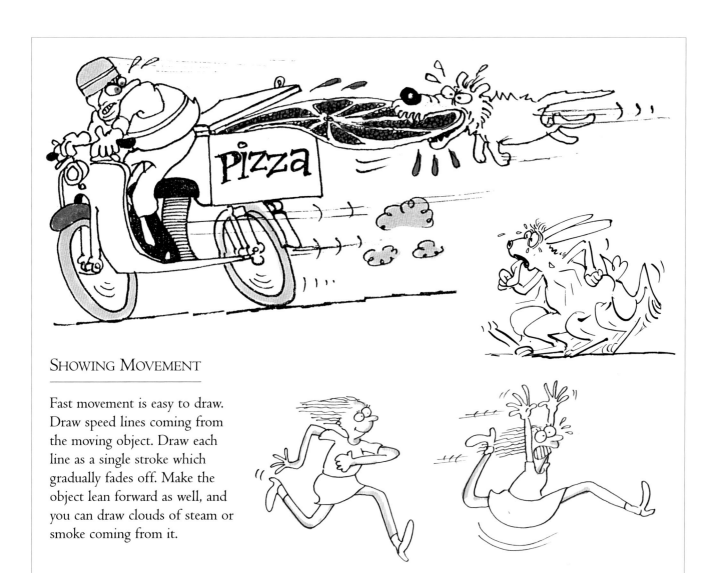

Showing Movement

Fast movement is easy to draw. Draw speed lines coming from the moving object. Draw each line as a single stroke which gradually fades off. Make the object lean forward as well, and you can draw clouds of steam or smoke coming from it.

Expressive Words

Both animals and humans can talk in cartoons. Animals can also make proper noises, such as "eek" for a mouse, and "miaow" for a cat. Words can also describe sound effects, such as "Boom" or "Crunch". If it is a loud or sudden sound effect you can draw in an exclamation mark, or two.

Bubbles and boxes

THE EASIEST WAY TO SHOW CARTOON characters speaking is by using speech bubbles, which come from their mouths. But you must draw them in the order they will be read, otherwise the story won't make sense.

HOW WE READ AND THINK

If your character has a lot to say, a big bubble will be needed, so make sure you have room for it without covering too much of the picture.

▲ Reading order
Read the question first, then the answer. Not all words need to be in bubbles, especially if they are more like sound effects, but make sure you leave a clear space in which to draw them.

▲ Thought bubbles
Thought bubbles are drawn like smoke clouds. They come from the brain, not the mouth, and are drawn slightly differently to speech bubbles.

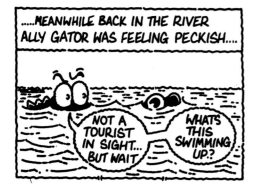

SPEECH BUBBLES

It is important to keep your story short, clear, and simple. Any words you need apart from speech can be put into boxes at the top and bottom of the picture. Bubbles are usually oval in shape. Keep them white with black lettering. Bubbles can also contain other sounds apart from words, such as loud music or singing.

A hard, jagged outline immediately tells you that the person speaking is either angry or talking very loudly.

Use capital letters. They are neater and easier to read.

Two people can say the same thing if you join them both to the same bubble.

Bold letters and an underline will emphasize an important word.

Use jagged bubbles for words that come from machines, like radios or robots.

The frame

▲ Frames
Look at existing comics to decide on a page size, before you plan your frames.

B Y NOW YOU SHOULD KNOW ALL YOU need to create great cartoon pictures, but each picture will usually need a frame around it. Also, the set of pictures that make up your story need to be laid out effectively on the page – this is called the layout of the pictures.

THE BOX STYLE

Remember that cartoons are read in the same way as a regular book, from left to right, starting at the top of the page. Choose the style of frame to suit your cartoon picture style.

▲ Frames
A loose, broken line.

▲ Frames
A hand drawn line.

▲ Frames
A line drawn with a ruler.

▲ Frames
A line with a drop shadow.

All of your frames don't have to be the same size. A big scene can be effective.

Lots of narrow, quick scenes can be shown by drawing smaller boxes close together.

Use a compass to draw a round scene and to curve the edges of the adjacent boxes.

PLANNING THE PAGE

Before you do any artwork, plan out each page as a simple doodle. Work out how many rows of pictures you can fit on, and where to put the title. Your final layout will also depend on what happens in the story!

If your pictures are varying shapes, make sure it is obvious which one the reader looks at next.

▼ Action comics
Pictures are really dynamic if things break out of the frame edge. Use "flash" or jagged frames for scenes such as battles.

The Story so Far

SO WHAT IS YOUR CARTOON CHARACTER GOING TO DO? YOU HAVE BUILT up its personality and lifestyle, and what it can and can't do. All you need now is a plot, whether it's a dramatic story, or just a brilliant joke that can be told in pictures.

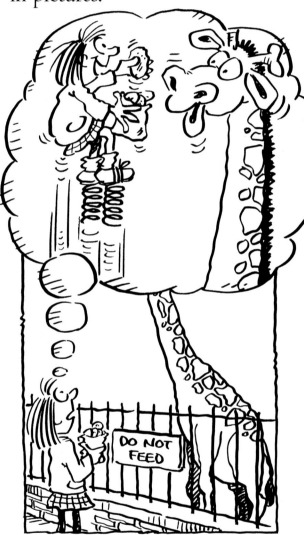

KEEPING THE READER INTERESTED The

Think of the reaction you want your readers to have. Do you want them to laugh or be sad, or possibly a bit of both? Whichever way, you need to keep the humor, action, and suspense, going until the end. That way your readers will keep on reading to find out what happens. Make them laugh or cry but make them wait!

▼ Thinking about it
As the comic strip is basically a picture story, try to think visually. Look out for comic situations that occur at home or school.

▲ Ideas
A simple idea is often best. Otherwise the reader can get confused about what is happening or who is who.

▲ Laughing
Make them roar with laughter.

▲ Crying
Bring tears to their eyes.

▲ Scared
Make their hair stand on end.

STORYLINE

The best way to plan your storyline is visually, as a cript (below), in which you can show the words and action separately. If you have an idea but keep getting stuck, make a "what if..." sheet and write down all the things that could happen, even the weirdest.

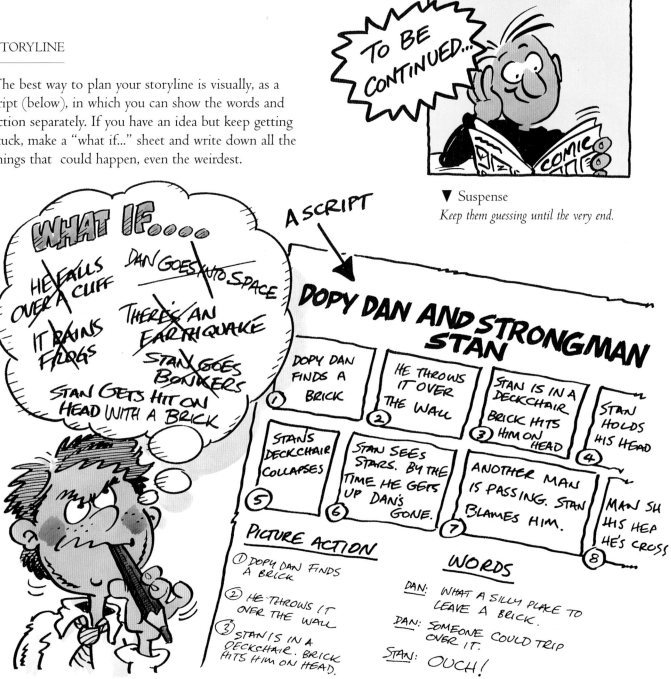

▼ Suspense
Keep them guessing until the very end.

153

Storyboards

 Y OU ARE FINALLY READY to start planning your actual cartoon strip. You do this by drawing a storyboard. This is a set of rough pictures which tell your story. Don't do them in too much detail to start with as you may want to make changes as you go.

▲ The storyboard
Your finished storyboard should have a series of finished pencil sketches and text in sequence. Show it to friends in case they suggest any changes before final artwork.

▼ Wallace and Grommit storyboards
On this spread are the storyboards of a famous animator, called Nick Park. They show how to create and work on a storyboard.

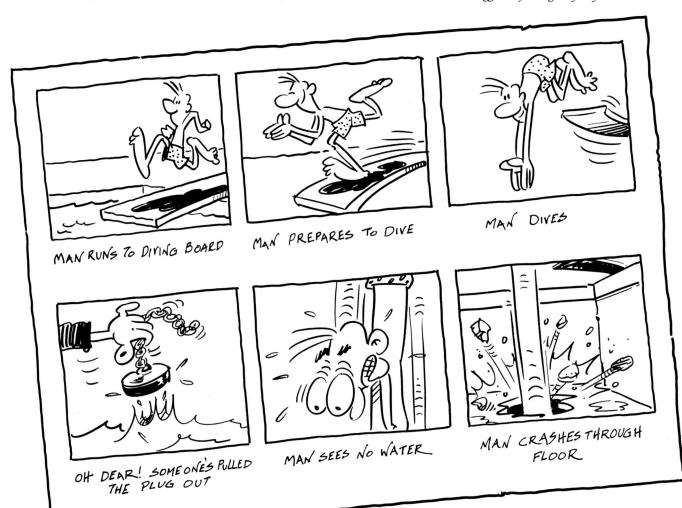

MAN RUNS TO DIVING BOARD

MAN PREPARES TO DIVE

MAN DIVES

OH DEAR! SOMEONE'S PULLED THE PLUG OUT

MAN SEES NO WATER

MAN CRASHES THROUGH FLOOR

How to make your Storyboard

Start by doing a rough sketch, then trace this neatly onto tracing paper, making any corrections as you go. Tack the separate frames lightly onto a board, and alter or add to the order until you are happy with everything. Then stick the pictures down, and you are ready to do the artwork.

DOG GOES FOR WALK

CAT SPIES DOG

CAT HAS IDEA

CAT MAKES LASOO

CAT LASOOS DOG

DOG HAS A LITTLE TRIP!

The artwork

DON'T BE TEMPTED TO RUSH YOUR final drawing. It does not have to be completed all in one go, although it is a good idea to work on it as often as you can, so that you don't loose track of how you are doing. Once your storyboard drawings are exactly right, you need to copy them onto your artwork paper or board.

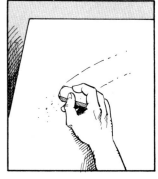

▲ Preparing the board
The surface of the board can be cleaned with an eraser to remove any greasy spots.

THE DRAWINGS

You may have to carefully copy all your drawings from your storyboard onto your artwork material. Or, tape the storyboard to the window, overlay thin artwork paper and trace the whole strip in pencil. Professionals use a lightbox.

▼ Scaling
Draw a grid over a drawing that is too big or too small. Then draw another grid to the correct size and copy square by square.

▲ Using pencils
Planning in pencil first allows you to make last minute changes and correct spelling.

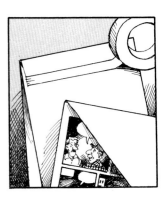

▲ Protective coverings
Always cover your artwork. Think how you would feel if all your hard work was ruined by tea!

ADDING COLOR

Next ink in (or use a fine felt pen) the whole strip, including all the words. Do the frame edges first, then the bubbles, words, and finally the pictures. Now you are ready to color in. It's a good idea to do one color at a time, that way it will be consistent throughout the strip. Your character should look the same in the last frame as in the first. If you make a mistake, cut out that frame or glue on a clean patch.

WHAT YOU NEED
Artwork paper or board
Glue or sticky tape
Pencils, ruler, eraser
Compass or round plate
Pens, crayons, paints, inks
layout paper

▲ Overlays
You can use overlays over your base artwork to add speech bubbles or another character.

The end

YOUR ARTWORK IS finished! Read through the story to check for any mistakes, and tidy up the artwork by erasing any pencil lines and clean up messy frame edges.

◄ Overlays
Professionals write the words on a tracing paper overlay. This is so that if their cartoon is published in another country, a different overlay can be easily done in another language.

Correction fluid can be used to white out a spelling mistake. Then draw over it.

LOOK AFTER YOUR ARTWORK

Artwork is easily damaged so protect it once it is finished. Tape it onto some card and put a cover on it, made from acetate or colored paper.

It's a good idea, before you show off your strip cartoon to your friends, to make a copy of it. Accidents can happen! Take it into a copy shop, and get a photocopy of it. If you can get a color copy done (but this is somewhat expensive) then you can show the color copy to your friends and keep the artwork safe.

► Display your artwork up
You can hang your finished cartoon strip up on a wall at home, or in your school. It is best not to hang artwork up in direct sunlight as some colors will fade. Felt tip pens and some inks fade quickest, while watercolors and colored crayons will last longer.

Original artwork also makes great presents, if you can bear to give all that hardwork away.

► Branch out!

If your family and friends like your cartoon character, you don't have to stick to cartoon strips. You can branch out into badges or stickers, or make up some puzzles or games featuring your favorite character. Ask your art teacher at school for helpful hints on how to get things printed, or if this is too expensive, you can make your own. T-shirts are fun to make, using a plain white shirt and special crayons for drawing on material.

◄ Expand your ideas

If your first cartoon strip was successful, or more importantly, if you enjoyed doing it, why not try to follow it up with a few more?

You have learnt where and how to seek inspiration for good ideas, so make it a habit to constantly keep your eyes and ears open for other cartoons. You will probably find that the more you draw the more ideas will come to you, and the quicker and easier it will become to bring them to life. If you lose interest in an idea though, it is best to leave it because if it starts to bore you it will certainly bore the people you show it to!

► Distribution!

If you do a number of cartoon strips, staple copies of then together to make a complete comic. You can design a cover for it as well, and see your name "in print." Who knows where it will end.

...Or the beginning

A CARTOON ANIMATION IS ALMOST the same as a cartoon strip, except that the characters really move and really speak. In animation you still have a scene, which then cuts to another, just like looking at a strip cartoon from frame to frame. Try simple animation by making a flick book, or a zoetrope, to start.

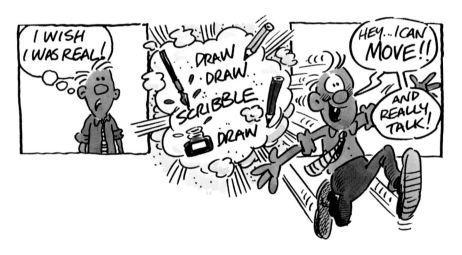

EARLY ANIMATION

At the turn of the twentieth-century comic strips and magazines were popular. This coincided with the development of animation. Some comic characters were brought to life in the early animations, and then many more were invented especially for animation. Some of the these were then turned into comic strip characters as well.

Dino Dinosaur
A panel from Winsor McCay's only known comic strip of the character Dino the Dinosaur, *drawn in 1909. Even in this small example, McCay's ability to suggest scale is apparent.*

▲ Animated characters
Comic cartoon characters were perfect for animation because they were simple. This made it easier to do the thousands of drawings needed to make them move even one step.

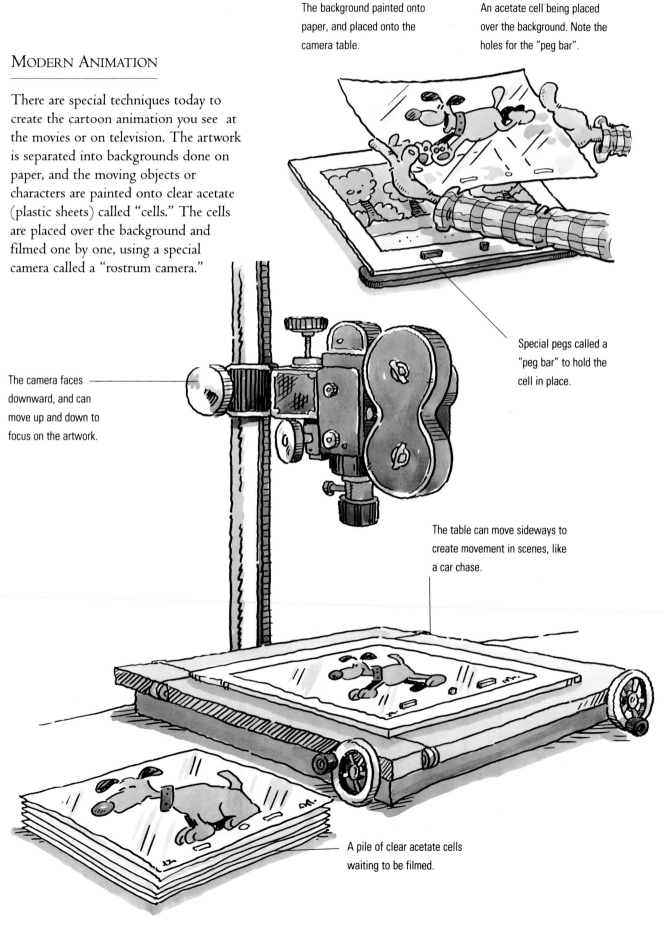

MODERN ANIMATION

There are special techniques today to create the cartoon animation you see at the movies or on television. The artwork is separated into backgrounds done on paper, and the moving objects or characters are painted onto clear acetate (plastic sheets) called "cells." The cells are placed over the background and filmed one by one, using a special camera called a "rostrum camera."

The background painted onto paper, and placed onto the camera table.

An acetate cell being placed over the background. Note the holes for the "peg bar".

Special pegs called a "peg bar" to hold the cell in place.

The camera faces downward, and can move up and down to focus on the artwork.

The table can move sideways to create movement in scenes, like a car chase.

A pile of clear acetate cells waiting to be filmed.

Back to the drawing board

PLANNING ANIMATION IS VERY SIMILAR to planning a strip cartoon. First you need your character, story, and script – but you can use ones you have already created – and then these need to be made into an animation storyboard, which is slightly different to a comic strip storyboard.

The frames need to be separate from the text, and all the same size and shape.

The text is written as action and dialog.

CREATING THE STORYBOARD

An animation storyboard is a series of finished sketches and frames, with text underneath to explain the action and showing the dialog. Unlike a comic strip storyboard, each frame needs to be the same size and shape, and there are no speech bubbles.

▶ Using a video
If you have access to a home video camera you can video the storyboard frame by frame to see how well it works.

DISCUSSING THE STORYBOARD

When your storyboard is finished it is a good idea to show it to friends or family – or anyone whose opinion you value – and see what they think.

Criticism is always hard to take, but it may be constructive. Or they may come up with many other ideas for cartoons, and ways to make your storyline even better than it is already.

MAN RUNS TO DIVING BOARD

MAN PREPARES TO DIVE

MAN DIVES

OH DEAR! SOMEONE'S PULLED THE PLUG OUT

MAN SEES NO WATER

MAN CRASHES THROUGH FLOOR

SOUNDS

Sounds are almost as important as pictures in animation. Your character will need a distinctive voice, as the way it sounds may be remembered as much as how it looks.

You may want to invent a catchphrase, or a special way that it talks and sings. Experiment with various voices yourself and record them onto a cassette.

▼ Different voices
Tape your pets for animal noises, or ask your friends to play different parts.

HOW DO I SOUND?

MORE LIKE A CAT THAN A DOG.

MAYBE I SHOULD STICK TO BARKING!

CLIP CLOP CLIP CLOP

◄ Sound effects
Think of ways to create sound effects for your story. There are standard ones, such as using coconut shells for horses hooves, and crumpling paper for rustling leaves. Experiment for yourself with everyday household things.

163

Making it move!

WHEN YOU WATCH A CARTOON movie, the projector makes 24 frames of film hit the screen every second, one after another. But you should do one drawing for every two frames, as the eye will see this as continuous movement when it is projected.

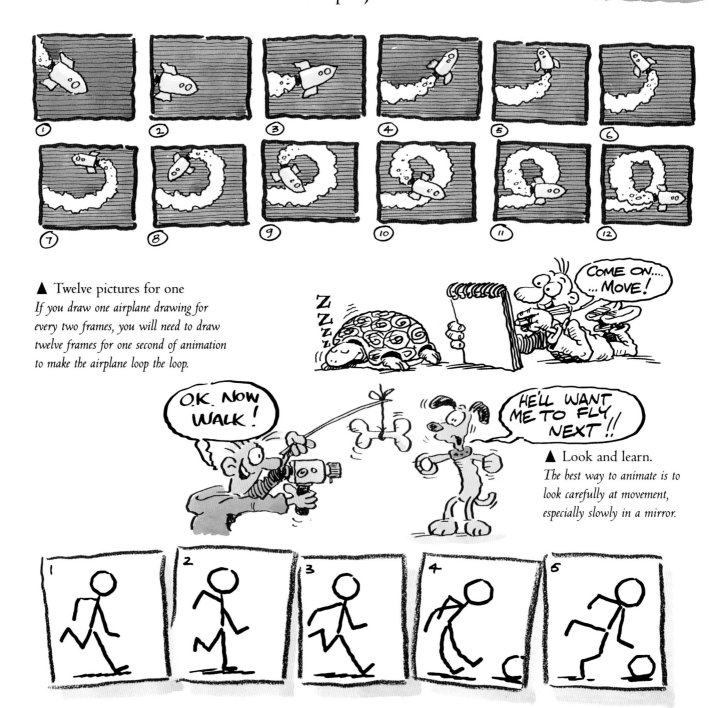

▲ Twelve pictures for one
If you draw one airplane drawing for every two frames, you will need to draw twelve frames for one second of animation to make the airplane loop the loop.

ZZZ

COME ON.... ...MOVE!

O.K. NOW WALK!

HE'LL WANT ME TO FLY NEXT!!

▲ Look and learn.
The best way to animate is to look carefully at movement, especially slowly in a mirror.

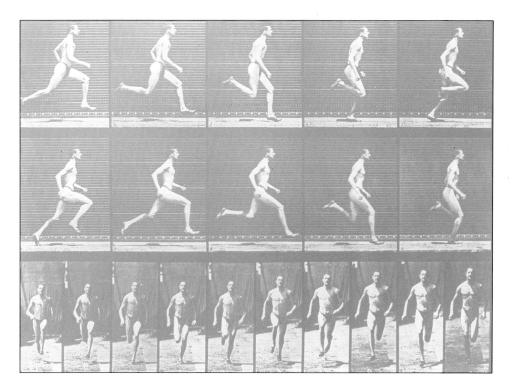

Muybridge.
*Muybridge (1830-1904)
began to study animal
locomotion in 1887. He
then moved onto human
movement. He took these
pictures by setting up a row
of cameras, which shot in
sequence one after the other. So
each frame in this picture was
taken by a separate camera.*

▶ **Key drawings**

*Try to draw the main positions of
the movement you want to animate,
especially the beginning, middle, and
end. These are called "key
drawings." The number of drawings
you do depends on how complicated
the movement is. For something
simple, like picking up a mug (left),
three would be enough.*

Start position
The man is just about to
pick the mug up.

Midway
He raises the mug
midway to his mouth.

End position
He reaches his mouth
and has a drink.

MOVEMENT

You can work out movement using stick people. Just do a series of small
drawings of a stick figure walking, running, kicking a football, or jumping
(see below). Then run your eye along them one by one and actually see
how the animation would work. If you blink between each frame, your eye
acts just like a camera.

▼ **Picture sequences.**
*Run your eye along the series of pictures on
the bottom of this spread. You will see it
does look as though he is running, kicking
the ball, slipping, and then falling over.*

The "inbetweens"

ANIMATION IS BASICALLY DOING A NUMBER of character drawings in "key positions," and then doing the drawings inbetween. This is called "inbetweening." The number of inbetween drawings, called "inbetweens," and "key drawings" will depend on how long you want the movement to last.

◀ Key drawings
Here are three key drawings for turning a head, which is slightly more complicated than lifting a cup. This is because the whole face moves as well. Number them, and do them on tracing paper.

▶ Start with the eyes
It is easiest to start with the eyes. Your new "inbetween" eye goes midway between the eyes labeled one and two.

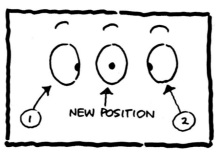

NEW POSITION

▲ Overlapping
Place drawing two over one, so that you can see both heads. Then put tracing paper over both, and draw a head inbetween them.

▼ Inbetweens
Keep doing drawings inbetween the key drawings, and re-number them all carefully. If you want a head to turn more slowly you can do extra inbetweens.

Start position with one inbetween before the mid-position.

IN BETWEENS

End position with one inbetween after the mid-position.

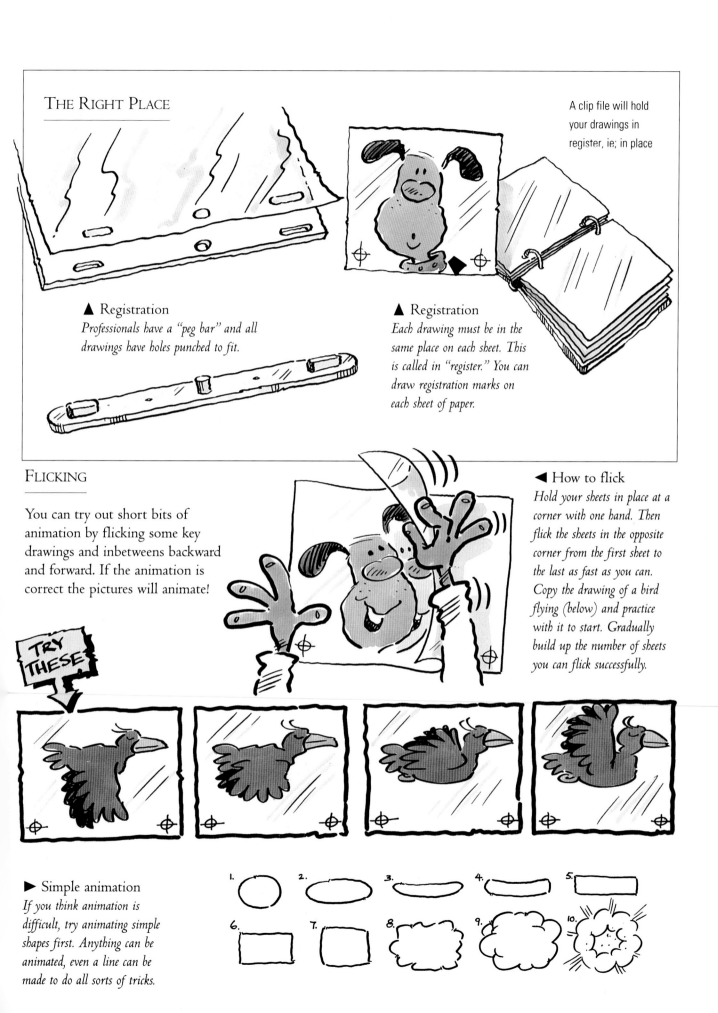

THE RIGHT PLACE

A clip file will hold your drawings in register, ie; in place

▲ Registration
Professionals have a "peg bar" and all drawings have holes punched to fit.

▲ Registration
Each drawing must be in the same place on each sheet. This is called in "register." You can draw registration marks on each sheet of paper.

FLICKING

You can try out short bits of animation by flicking some key drawings and inbetweens backward and forward. If the animation is correct the pictures will animate!

◄ How to flick
Hold your sheets in place at a corner with one hand. Then flick the sheets in the opposite corner from the first sheet to the last as fast as you can. Copy the drawing of a bird flying (below) and practice with it to start. Gradually build up the number of sheets you can flick successfully.

TRY THESE

► Simple animation
If you think animation is difficult, try animating simple shapes first. Anything can be animated, even a line can be made to do all sorts of tricks.

1. 2. 3. 4. 5.
6. 7. 8. 9. 10.

Shortcuts

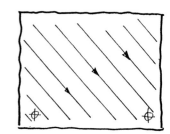

I F YOU LOOK AT THINGS THAT MOVE, YOU'LL notice that many actions are made up of a set of movements that are repeated. Look at a side view of someone walking – once they have put one leg forward and then the other, the rest is a repeat of the same action. Animators call this a "cycle" of action.

CYCLES

"Cycles" really help animators, as only one set of movements needs to be drawn, and these can be filmed over and over again. Any movement in which there is a pattern can become a cycle, but not random action.

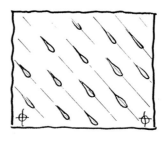

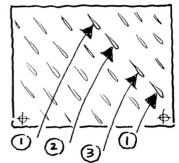

▼ Butterfly flying cycle
Here is a cycle of butterfly wings, in six steps. The cycle of action goes from steps one to six, and then back to one again, and so on.

▲ Raining overlays
Draw the direction of the rain on overlay one; draw some rain on overlay two; draw more rain farther down on overlay three.

▼ Simple walking cyle
This is a simple walk cycle. Notice that the arms, head, and the rest of the body all move as well as the legs. A more realistic walk cycle would need 16 cycles.

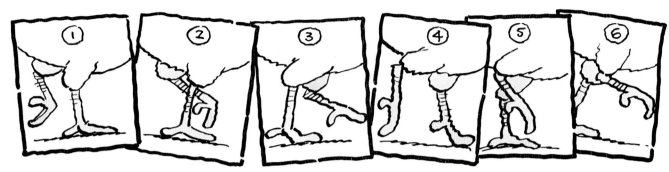

▲ Chicken walk

Chicken legs are a good way to practice walk cycles. Do each leg in a different color so you know which is which. With all action cycles draw your key positions and then as many inbetweens as you want.

► Waving

An arm wave is drawn as a cycle moving from bottom to top, then top to bottom. You would film from one to five, five to one, then start again.

Work out a walk cycle in stick legs first. As with the chicken legs draw different colored legs.

Backgrounds

IN ANIMATION THE characters and the backgrounds need to be separate pieces of artwork, so that the position of the character can be seen over the same background scene. Although the background is a separate piece of artwork, it should still relate to the characters and action, so they work as a whole.

SLOTTING TOGETHER

You can place more than one "cell" on the background artwork, so that different characters and objects can be included to add variety to the background, and to give the impression of movement.

▲ Character and background work together
Both the background and the character show that it is a windy day. They fit together so well that you can't guess they were separate.

A background

An acetate cell with the character painted on

Another cell with a different animation on

Backgrounds and both cells put together

► Panning backgrounds
When you see a chase in an animated movie or program, the characters really look as though they are running. In fact they are animated as if they are running on the spot. Behind them a long scene called a panning background is moved to create the impression of speed.

► A city scene
You can add extra interest to a city scene by painting different vehicles and pedestrians on separate acetate cells and varying them.

▲ A country scene
A country scene may look slightly bare with only open fields. So add different animals, farmers, or a tractor to the scene. They do not have to stay in the far background; this horse could gallop right up to the gate for added impact.

Flick books

BECAUSE ANIMATION IS EXPENSIVE TO GET onto film or video, you can only practice bits of it for now. Making a flick book will give you a chance to see your pictures move. You can either buy some small plain paper pads, or make your own. Try something short and easy at first in pencil, so that you can correct any little details that don't work.

MAKING A FLICKBOOK

1 *Use fairly stiff paper and cut it up into small rectangles. Any size will do but small ones are easier to flick. Cut 25 to 30 pieces.*

2 *Do the animation drawings on each piece. Number each one on the back in case they get muddled up. Keep it fairly simple. It is best not to bother with a background as you will have to copy it onto every page.*

3 *The cartoon must be in the same place on each page for them to animate properly. Leave a space on the left hand side for your glue or staples. To work out the animation, either start on the first piece of paper and change the picture as you go along or draw a "master" drawing with the different positions marked on it. You can trace these off using carbon paper or rub pencil on the back.*

*Actual size for
you to trace off.*

4 *Write your title on the first page and then arrange them in the
right order. Staple or glue each sheet together. Use sticky tape to
tape over the spine. This will keep your pages neatly together.*

5 *To see your animation come to life, hold the book in your left
hand and flick with your right. You may need to practice this
a few times until you get it absolutely right.*

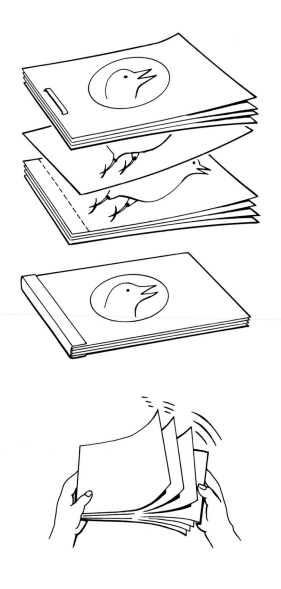

Zoetrope

The zoetrope was a Victorian toy in which strips of pictures were put, then viewed through slits as the zoetrope was spun around. The slits act like a movie projector. Each one shows the eye one picture at a time very quickly so that they become animated.

HOW TO MAKE A ZOETROPE

1 *Draw a circle on the card with a compass, and cut it out. Make a cross slit in the center as shown. If you use a plate, measure the distance round the edge to work out how long to make the wall.*

2 *Take your card and draw and cut out the wall, making ten evenly spaced slits. These should be about 5mm (1/4 inch) wide. Make it in sections if your card isn't long enough. Cut out tab shapes at the bottom and on one edge of the wall, as shown in the diagram.*

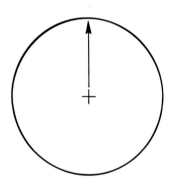

3 *Bend the tabs inwards and drop in the base to make sure it is the right size. If it is too big, trim it to size. Put some glue on the upper surfaces of the tabs. Then, glue the wall to make a cylinder. Drop the base down into the cylinder again and this time glue it to the tabs.*

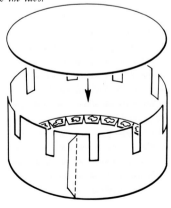

The next stage is making the animation. Here are some examples of the kind of drawings you could do.

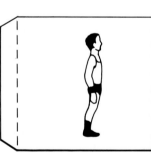

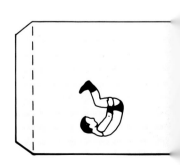

MAKING THE ANIMATION

Because a zoetrope is round, and the strip of pictures will be viewed continuously, they must show an animation "cycle" — an animation that keeps on repeating itself without any gaps.

You can make as many animations as you like, but do one first to check it's the right size.

Keep your image fairly simple to begin with.

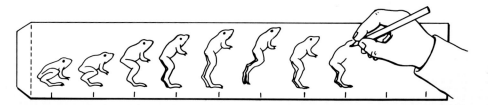

▼ Cylinder
Cut a strip of paper the same length as the wall but only half as high. Put ten marks spaced the same distance apart as the wall slits. Draw an image above each mark.

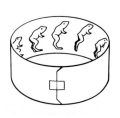

▼ Fixing together.
Before you stick both ends of your strip together, check that it fits neatly into your zoetrope. Push a pencil through the slit.

▼ Using the zoetrope.
Turn the pencil to spin the zoetrope and look through the slits. It needs to be well balanced to turn evenly.

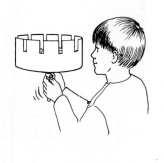

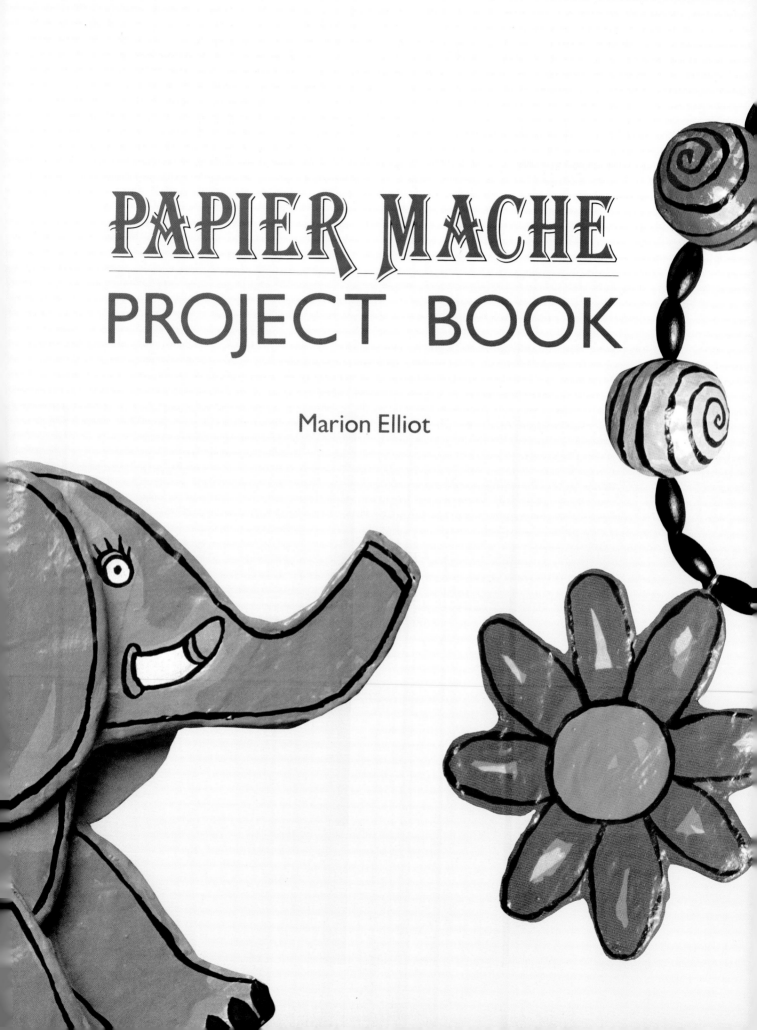

PAPIER MACHE
PROJECT BOOK

Marion Elliot

CONTENTS

Papier Mache Project Book

WHAT IS PAPIER-MACHE?

Every year, millions of tons of waste paper are thrown away – here are lots of fun and creative ways of recycling some of it!

Papier-mâché, which is French for "chewed paper," is an exciting way to make something new out of waste paper, and there are two main methods of making it – pulping and layering.

For the pulping method, small pieces of paper are soaked in water until they disintegrate. Then they are mashed into a pulp, drained, squeezed almost dry, and mixed with glue. Watered-down white craft glue is most suitable for this purpose. The resulting pulp can be pressed into greased molds or used to add details to objects made by the layering method. If small amounts of pulp are needed, you can take a pasted strip of paper and scrunch it between your fingers to form a pellet of pulp.

The second method, layering, is the main method used in this book for making papier-mâché. This involves

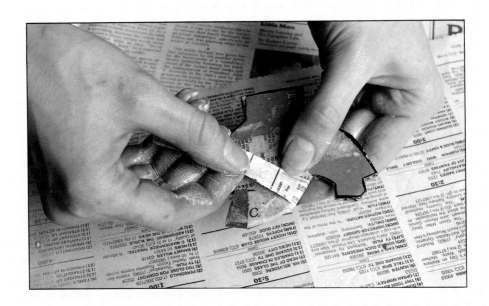

sticking strips of torn paper together and results in a very tough, but light, substance. Sometimes pulp is used to add details to some of the projects.

There are more than 20 projects for you to try, but these are only the beginning. You'll have plenty of your own ideas once you start work, and as your confidence grows and you become more competent, you'll probably be keen to experiment with your new skills. You might even like to adapt the projects to reflect your own hobbies and interests.

The first two sections describe all the materials and techniques you will need to make papier-mâché. These are followed by the projects themselves, with ideas for special events and occasions, toys to make, jewelry to wear, boxes and frames of various kinds, and, to start you off, a simple plate and a bowl.

It is a good idea to read the techniques section thoroughly before you embark on any projects so that you become familiar with the basic skills required and the materials you will need. Even if things seem a little messy at first, it is worth persevering – you will find that it is great fun making your own creations from papier-mâché!

GETTING STARTED

What you need

Paper

First, and most obviously, you will need paper! All sorts of paper are suitable, and different papers will give different results. Collect a variety of papers – newspaper, computer printout paper, brown wrapping paper and even telephone directories – and test them for suitability. The lighter and thinner the paper you use, the smoother your finished objects will be.

For layering, where strips of paper are pasted on top of each other, it is best to use newspaper, as the layers bond together well and stick smoothly. Nearly everyone reads newspapers, so you shouldn't have any trouble collecting some! For pulping, where small pieces of paper are soaked in water, squeezed almost dry and mixed with glue, you can use almost any kind of paper, but do avoid all paper that is waxed or has a waterproof finish – this will look shiny – as it is not possible to break it down by soaking in water. As a general rule, the smoother and whiter the paper you use, the finer the pulp will be. Experiment with a variety of papers to discover which effects you like best.

Glue

So, having collected all your paper, you will need glue to stick it together. The best choice is cold-water wallpaper paste – be careful to use a brand that is nontoxic though. Wallpaper paste is easy to mix, and leftovers can be stored in an airtight container. If you spill some on your clothes, it won't stain, and it washes out easily. An alternative to wallpaper paste is sticky white craft glue. If you use it for making papier-mâché, you will need to dilute it first, by adding about twice as much water as glue. This glue dries more quickly than wallpaper paste and results in stronger papier-mâché, but it does have one big disadvantage: splashes won't wash out of clothes, carpets, or upholstery once they have dried, and you could become highly unpopular if you accidentally spill some! Again, if you do use white glue, remember to choose a nontoxic brand.

Apart from undiluted white glue, which is used in some projects to stick pieces of cardboard together, several projects also need nontoxic, strong, clear adhesive. Several brands of clear glue are suitable, but never use an epoxy-resin glue.

HELPFUL HINT . . .

If possible, use different colored paper for each layer of papier-mâché – it will enable you to see if you've completely covered the object with one layer before you begin the next and help to prevent uneven patches.

Equipment

Now that you have your main ingredients, you will also need some basic equipment. You will probably already have some **rulers** and **pencils**. Plastic rulers are fine for measuring pieces of cardboard, transferring measurements and so on, but when you have to cut straight lines, you should use a metal ruler. Your plastic ruler will eventually become chipped if you cut against it with a craft knife.

To mix the glue, whether you are using wallpaper paste or white glue, you will need a **large plastic bowl**. A sink bowl is perfect, although it is a good idea to keep it to one side reserved especially for glue and to avoid using it for washing the dishes in, too.

A **craft knife** is very useful for cutting cardboard, especially if you are using the heavy-duty kind. However, you must be very, very careful with these knives, as their blades are extremely sharp. Always get an adult to help you at this stage in a project to prevent accidents.

You will need some **petroleum jelly** to grease molds before you put papier-mâché into them. The jelly creates a barrier between the mold and the paper, allowing the paper shape to be removed easily when it is dry – rather like a cake from a cake pan.

Modeling clay is very useful for making large, three-dimensional items such as puppet heads. You can make a sort of mold for the head by modeling it in clay first and then covering it with several layers of papier-mâché. Allow the paper to dry thoroughly, and then cut it open and remove the clay. Join the paper halves back together with strips of pasted paper. You can add facial features – ears and a nose, for example – to the head with small pellets of paper pulp.

A **palette-knife** with a thin blade is useful for helping to remove dry papier-mâché shapes from the sides of molds and for prising clay from the inside of finished pieces.

A **wire cake rack** is ideal for drying smaller items because it allows air to circulate freely around them. The pieces can be removed quite easily when they are dry.

Scissors are handy for cutting around shapes made from thin cardboard. Don't, however, use scissors to cut paper into strips – it should always be torn.

The finished projects are decorated with **poster paint**. There is a wide choice of colors available, but remember to check that you are using a nontoxic brand. The same applies to the **black India ink** that is used to outline designs – always use a nontoxic brand.

Masking tape is used in many of the projects to hold sections of cardboard together while they are drying. You can peel the tape from the card once the glue has set, but it will give extra strength to your constructions if you leave it in place and simply paper over it.

Cardboard is used to make the basic structure in several projects. Two different weights are used: **heavy corrugated cardboard** for larger items like the puppet theater, where strength is needed to avoid warping, and **thinner card** for such projects as the Christmas decorations, earrings, and brooch. Empty boxes from the supermarket, electrical goods stores, and the like are ideal for heavy cardboard as long as they are clean and uncreased.

Clear gloss varnish was used to seal most of the projects in this book and to give them an attractive, shiny surface. Use a nontoxic brand. It is possible to buy a type of varnish that is made specifically for paper crafts such as papier-mâché, and this is quite safe. As with all the paints, glues, and inks used for these projects, an educational supplier or art store with a children's section will be able to tell you which brands are suitable. However, if you use a varnish that can only be cleaned off brushes with turpentine, ask an adult to help you, as turpentine can be dangerous if it is handled carelessly.

HELPFUL HINT . . .

Always use nontoxic glues and paints. Ask the store clerk for advice if you're in any doubt.

Techniques

Before you start any of the projects, read through all the instructions carefully to check how long the project will take you – many stages need to dry out overnight, so it is best to plan ahead.

Tearing paper

The length and width of your paper strips will vary according to what you are making. Pieces up to 3 in. (7.5cm) wide can be used if you are covering large, flat surfaces, but you will often find that you need much smaller pieces, some only as large as postage stamps.

When you are tearing up paper, bear in mind that it has a grain, like fabric, and it will tear much more easily in one direction than the other, usually – though not always – from the top to the bottom. Never cut paper into strips with scissors; this will give it a blunt, hard edge, which will show up when your object is painted and varnished.

Tear along the correct grain of the paper, as in the top picture. You can see, in the bottom picture, what happens if you do it the wrong way!

HELPFUL HINT . . .

Wash your hands when you have been tearing up newspaper. You will be surprised at how much ink comes off the paper!

Gluing

Your strips of paper should be covered on both sides with wallpaper paste or watered-down white glue. You can use your fingers or a brush to apply the glue, but don't use too much, or your object will take a long time to dry.

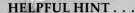

HELPFUL HINT . . .

Cover your worktop or table with old newspaper to prevent it from getting marked with splashes of glue or paint. Best of all, use a plastic sheet, which can be wiped clean when you have finished work for the day.

Using a mold

All sorts of objects can be used as molds for papier-mâché. Bowls, plates, and dishes are ideal. Always smear petroleum jelly over the mold before you use it, or it will be very difficult to remove the dried paper shape. Cardboard is also a good "mold" or base – but it will be left inside the paper as a permanent part of the structure. Several layers can be built up on top of cardboard to make a good, strong base.

Drying

The time each piece will take to dry will depend on its size and the number of layers of papier-mâché you have used. Usually, 24 hours is adequate for a cardboard shape with two or three layers of paper on it, but a balloon with eight layers of papier-mâché may take up to 3 days to dry. Use a warm place to dry your papier-mâché.

186

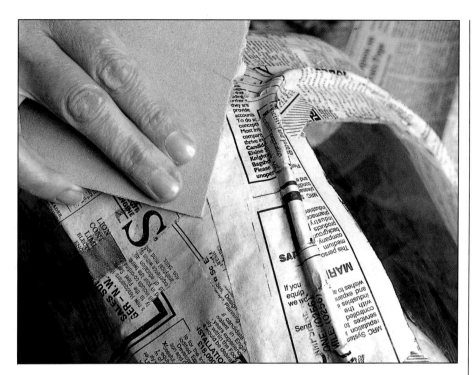

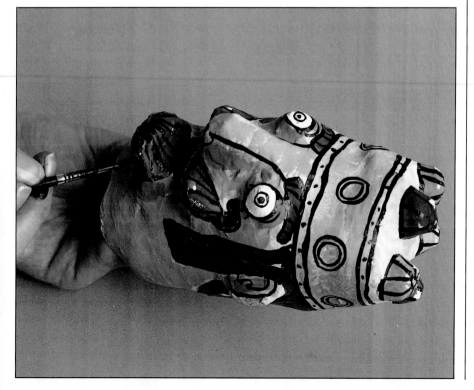

HELPFUL HINT . . .

Wear a plastic apron or a pair of overalls when you make papier-mâché – it can be quite messy.

Sanding

When your papier-mâché is dry, you should lightly rub down the surface with fine sandpaper. This will remove any wrinkles in the paper and give you a smoother surface to paint on.

Priming

Use two coats of white paint to prime the surface of your papier-mâché. This will cover up newsprint effectively, gives a bright ground to paint on, and will make your colors seem more luminous. You must let the first coat dry before adding the second, or the paint may crack. If this happens, let the paint dry, sand it back to the paper, and start again. Always use nontoxic paint.

Decorating

When you have primed the papier-mâché, it can be decorated with poster paint. You will have to thin the paint with water, and you will probably need to use two coats to achieve a good, deep color. Black India ink, which is waterproof, can be used to accentuate the painted designs. Apply it with a thin paintbrush and use a nontoxic brand.

PLATE & BOWL

These two projects will introduce you to the basic techniques you will be using to make papier-mâché. The first, a plate, involves very simple layering into a greased mold, while the second, a bowl, requires the use of two molds.

The plate shape is left quite plain, and when its edges have been sealed with paper strips to stop it from "unraveling," it is decorated and varnished. The outside of the bowl is decorated with small lumps of papier-mâché, and the rim, middle and base, are trimmed with cord to make it looks sturdier.

The molds are simple household items – bowls and dishes – that you might find in the kitchen. They are very plain, but spend a little time and thought to discover combinations of molds that will look good together and produce interesting and original results.

You could even use molds in the shape of fish and animals, or items like heart-shaped cake pans, but be sure to ask permission before you start work or you may be banned from the kitchen!

Plate

This is a very simple project to teach you the basics of papier-mâché, and it involves the process known as layering, by which strips of paper are laid on top of one another to form a strong paper shell.

The plate is decorated in bold, cheerful colors, and it is sealed with two coats of clear gloss varnish. Although you should not put wet things on it, the plate would hold fruit or something similar, or it could be hung on a wall as a decorative plaque. You could make several, painting them to match the color scheme of a bedroom or the kitchen.

YOU WILL NEED

A plastic plate ● Petroleum jelly ● Paper ● Wallpaper paste or watered-down white glue ● Blunt knife or palette-knife ● Scissors ● Fine sandpaper ● Poster paints ● Black India ink ● Clear gloss varnish

---

Making the plate

1 Grease the plate you are using as your mold with a thin layer of petroleum jelly. This will make it easy to release the finished plate shape from the mold when it has dried. Tear the paper into strips about 1 in. (2.5cm) wide and long enough to stretch across the plate with about 1 in. (2.5cm) hanging over the edge at each side.

2 Coat the first strip of paper with wallpaper paste or watered-down white glue and lay it in the mold, smoothing out any creases or air bubbles. Continue to lay pasted strips of paper across the plate, covering the edge of the last strip you have put in position with the new piece.

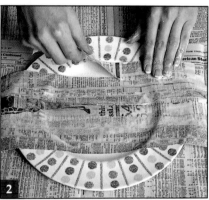

3 When you have completely covered the mold with the first layer of pasted paper, lay a second layer of strips across the plate, in the opposite direction to the first layer. This will guarantee that the papier-mâché is good and strong. Continue to cover the plate with layers of pasted paper in this way until you have completed eight layers. Then leave your plate to dry for 48 hours in a warm, dry place.

4 When the papier-mâché is dry, put the blade of a blunt knife or of a palette-knife under the edge of the paper where it meets the rim of the mold and gently prize it away. Because you greased the plastic plate with petroleum jelly, the paper should come away quite easily. Your paper shape will probably be a bit damp underneath, so lay it down in a warm place to dry for a few hours.

5 When the papier-mâché is dry, use a pair of scissors to trim the edge neatly back to within ¼ in. (5mm) of the rim.

6 The cut edge will need sealing. Take a strip of paper about 1 in. (2.5cm) wide, cover it with paste or glue and carefully wrap it over the edge, tearing it off at the other side. Repeat this process until you have sealed all around the edges of your plate. Leave the plate to dry overnight on a wire cake rack.

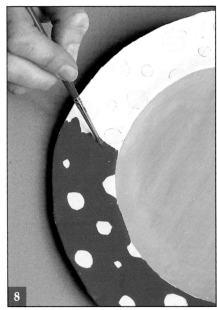

7 Rub down the dry plate gently with fine sandpaper, paying special attention to the sealed edge, which may be a bit lumpy. When it is smooth, give your plate two coats of white paint, allowing the first coat to dry before you add the second. Let the paint dry for an hour or so after the second coat is applied.

HELPFUL HINT . . .

Don't be tempted to leave papier-mâché to dry in strong sunlight – it may become warped.

8 Draw a design on the plate with pencil and start to fill in the color. You will probably have to use two layers of paint to get a good, deep color. Don't forget to paint the back as well!

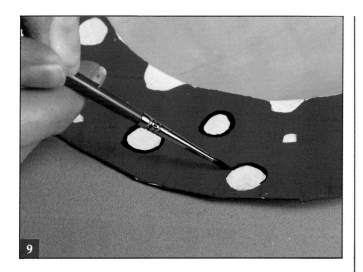

9 Allow your painted plate to dry for 4 hours and then outline your design with black India ink. Let the plate dry overnight.

10 Give the finished plate two coats of clear gloss varnish. You will probably have to paint the front of the plate and let it dry before you can varnish the back. Allow the first coat of varnish on each side of the plate to dry before you add the second. Remember to wash your varnishing brush with soap and water when you have finished.

Barnacle Bowl

*In addition to using some of the basic techniques involved in making papier-mâché, this bowl is made from **two** separate pieces which have to be joined together. The main part of the bowl is made by laying thin strips of paper in a greased mold, while a smaller mold is used to make the "foot" that the bowl stands on. The bowl and foot are joined together with strips of papier-mâché, and their edges are bound with cord and covered to create a rim.*

YOU WILL NEED

Two plastic bowls, one about 8 in. (20cm) in diameter, one about 3 in. (7.5cm) in diameter ● Petroleum jelly ● Paper ● Wallpaper paste or watered-down white glue ● Blunt knife or palette-knife ● Scissors ● Preshrunk piping cord ● Masking tape ● White glue (undiluted) ● Fine sandpaper ● Poster paints ● Black India ink ● Clear gloss varnish

The body of the bowl illustrated is made in a plastic bowl with a diameter of about 8 in. (20cm), and the foot is made from a straight-sided margarine tub. Whatever bowls you choose, make sure that they look balanced together and as if they are meant to be joined.

The bowl is decorated with little pellets of paper pulp, which are applied in a regular pattern and painted in bright colors. Paper pulp is a very effective method of adding decoration to papier-mâché items, and quite ornate designs can be built up very quickly so that even rather plain shapes can be transformed into exciting articles.

The bowl can be used to hold a variety of dry objects, especially fruit, although you may want to choose varieties that don't clash with your color scheme! Don't keep wet things in it, however – it won't be waterproof, and you may spoil the varnished surface.

Making the bowl

1 Grease the insides of the molds with a little petroleum jelly so that the papier-mâché shapes can be easily removed when they are dry. Tear your paper into strips 1–1½ in. (2.5–4cm) wide and long enough to fit the bowl from one side to the other with about 1 in. (2.5cm) of excess paper on each edge. Begin to lay your pasted paper in the bowl, making sure that the strips lie flat against the walls. Continue to lay the paper in the bowl, covering the edge of the strip you have just put in place with the next strip. You may have to fan the strips out slightly as you move around the bowl so that the papier-mâché does not crease.

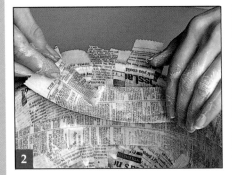

2 When you have finished the first layer of paper, start the second, laying the strips at right angles to the first layer, to give a good, strong bowl. Add eight layers of strips. Leave the papier-mâché to dry in a warm place for 48 hours.

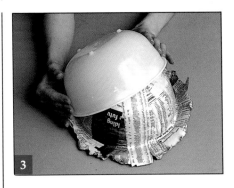

3 When the surface of the bowl feels dry, gently insert the blade of a blunt knife or a palette-knife between the paper and mold, and ease the paper shells away from the sides. Lay the shape upside-down in a warm place to dry for a few hours.

4 The edges of your paper shapes will need sealing to stop them from coming apart. Use scissors to trim the excess paper back to within ¼ in. (5mm) of the edge of your bowl.

5 Then take a pasted strip of paper, about 1 in. (2.5cm) wide, and fully overlap the cut edge, tearing off the excess strip as you reach the back of the bowl each time. One layer of binding strips will be enough.

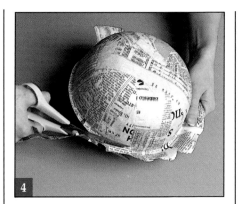

6 Leave the bound edges to dry and then place the piping cord around the outside edges of the bowl, pushing the cord right up against the lip of the rim. Secure the ends of the cord together with masking tape and tape the cord in place at several points around the rim. Then cover the cord with strips of paper, exactly as you did when you sealed the cut edges. Cover the cord with three layers of papier-mâché, and let the bowl dry for 24 hours.

Making the foot

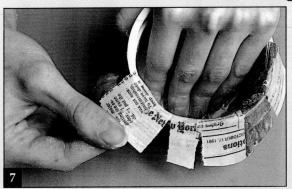

7 Grease the inside of the foot and lay in the strips of paper as you did in the bowl. Lay each of the 8 layers in at different angles to one another, and leave to dry out for 48 hours, before easing the paper cast out of the mold.

8 Trim back the paper as in step 4 and bind the edges with small pieces of paper. Leave to dry and then wrap the cord around the rim as in step 6. Secure it and seal with 3 layers of papier-mâché and allow it to dry for 24 hours.

Joining the foot to the bowl

9 Now dab some undiluted white glue on the top of the foot section and position it squarely under the body. Tape the two together with masking tape and leave the glue to dry for a couple of hours. Place a piece of cord around the join (a), tape it in place, and cover it with three layers of papier-mâché (b). Leave the bowl to dry for 24 hours.

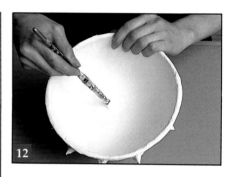

10 When your bowl is completely dry, you can make it more ornate with paper pulp additions if you wish. To make the "barnacles," take a strip of paper about 1 in. (2.5cm) wide and 8 in. (20cm) long. Coat it with glue and squash it into a pellet.

11 Then simply press the pellet firmly to the outside of your bowl to fix it, repeating the process as many times as you wish. If you want the "barnacles" to have a smooth surface, cover them with very short, thin strips of paper, say ¼ in. (5mm) wide and 1½ in. (4cm) long. Leave your bowl to dry for 24 hours.

12 When it is dry, smooth the bowl with fine sandpaper and paint it with two coats of white poster paint, allowing the first coat to dry thoroughly before adding the next.

13 Paint the rope bands in colors that contrast with the body – you will probably need two coats of color to cover the white paint completely – then paint the "barnacles" in whatever colors appeal to you.

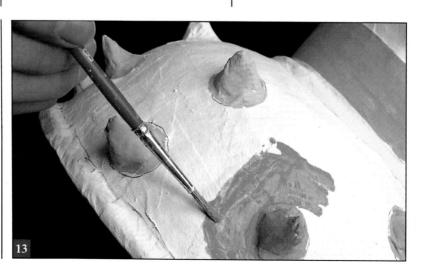

14 Let the paint dry for 3–4 hours and paint contrasting black ink lines on your bowl using a fine paint-brush. Leave the bowl to dry for 24 hours.

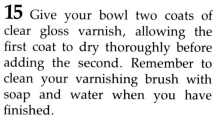

15 Give your bowl two coats of clear gloss varnish, allowing the first coat to dry thoroughly before adding the second. Remember to clean your varnishing brush with soap and water when you have finished.

JEWELRY

Lots of different kinds of jewelry can be made in papier-mâché – small, neat brooches and earrings as well as over-the-top necklaces and bangle bracelets. Make a selection and wear them according to your mood! All the items shown here involve the basic papier-mâché techniques, and you can make some stunning pieces by combining methods. Papier-mâché jewelry will make lovely presents for birthdays, Christmas, Mother's Day, or any special occasion, and your family and friends will be thrilled to receive something made especially for them.

You can, of course, personalize jewelry. You could write your name or a special message on a brooch or decorate bracelets and necklaces to match special outfits or costumes. The possibilities are endless – have fun trying some of them!

You will need what are known as "findings" for some of your jewelry. Findings are what you use to finish a piece – brooch pins, earring clips, necklace fastenings, and so on. They are inexpensive and can be bought from craft and hobby stores and from jewelry suppliers. If you are making earrings for pierced ears and are allergic to metal, you can buy silver and gold hooks, although these are more expensive.

Earrings

These bright flower earrings look very attractive, and their design matches the daisy necklace featured later in this section, so you could make a set by decorating both pieces in the same way. Although they are quite large, these earrings are very light, and you could make them even larger or longer without weighing your ears down. Other motifs that would look good include hearts, stars, and fish. You could make several pairs when you have learned the basic technique. The earrings are attached to the ears by clips, which are stuck to the backs of the yellow disks with strong glue.

EARRINGS TEMPLATES (*Thin cardboard*)

Making the earrings

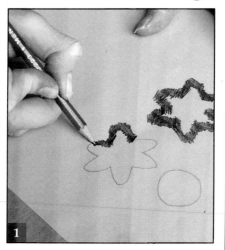

1 Trace the earring shapes from the pattern above and transfer them to the thin cardboard.

2 Cut around the shapes with a craft knife or scissors. **Ask an adult to help you if you use a craft knife, because it will have a very sharp edge.** Paint your cutout shapes with one coat of watered-down white glue. Lay them on a wire cake rack for 4 hours to dry.

YOU WILL NEED

Tracing paper • Thin cardboard approximately 4 x 4 in. (10 x 10cm) • Craft knife or scissors • Wallpaper paste or watered-down white glue • Paper • Fine sandpaper • Poster paints • Black India ink • Clear gloss varnish • Darning needle • White glue (undiluted) • 2 pairs of earring hooks and eyes • Strong, clear glue • 1 pair of clip fastenings • Small pair of pliers

---

HELPFUL HINT . . .

Knives, especially craft knives, can be dangerous. Always hold what you are cutting very carefully, and cut away from you. Better still, ask an adult to help you.

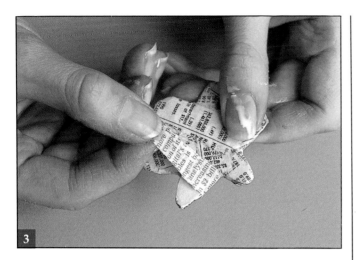

3 Using small strips of paper, about ½ in. × 2 in. (12mm × 5cm), cover the earring shapes with three layers of pasted paper. Work carefully around each petal, making sure that your papier-mâché does not become too lumpy so that it will have a smooth finish. Lay the papered shapes on a cake rack to dry for 24 hours.

4 When the shapes are completely dry, smooth them down lightly with fine sandpaper and coat them with two layers of white paint, allowing the first to dry before you add the second. Draw the center of the daisy on your flower shapes. The petal outlines and swirls will be drawn freehand on top of the poster paint later with black India ink.

5 Start to fill in the color. The petals were painted light blue, and then, when this coat was dry, they were painted again in violet, with the light blue allowed to show through in patches. The disks have been given two coats of yellow paint.

When you have painted all the pieces, allow them to dry for 4 hours.

6 Then, using a fine paintbrush, carefully draw in the black outlines and swirls. Let the earrings dry

overnight, then varnish the fronts with clear gloss varnish. Lay the pieces (varnished side up!) on a wire cake rack to dry. Varnish the backs and allow them to dry again. Repeat the process so that the fronts and backs have two coats of varnish.

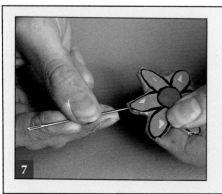

7 When the second coat of varnish is dry, make a small hole with a darning needle in the top of the petal section and in the bottom of the disk. Dab a little undiluted white glue into the holes. Push an earring hook section into the hole in each flower and an eye into each disk.

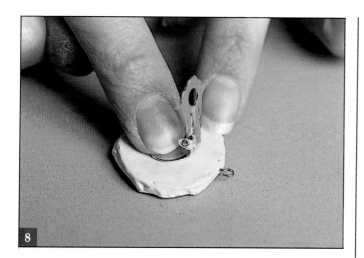

8 Dab some strong, clear glue onto the earring clips, and position one on the back of each disk. Press the disk and clip together firmly, and let all the earring pieces dry overnight.

9 Loop the hook into the eye, joining the disk and the flower, and close the opening with a small pair of pliers. Your earrings are now ready to wear!

Bracelets

Bracelets can be as simple or as ornate as you like. They can be made for special occasions and decorated accordingly, or they can be worn as bright, cheerful, everyday accessories. Here are two simple examples for you to make, which can be adapted to any occasion. You might like a perfectly plain circle, decorated with vibrant patterns and color, or you might prefer a more sophisticated, but simply decorated, bracelet.

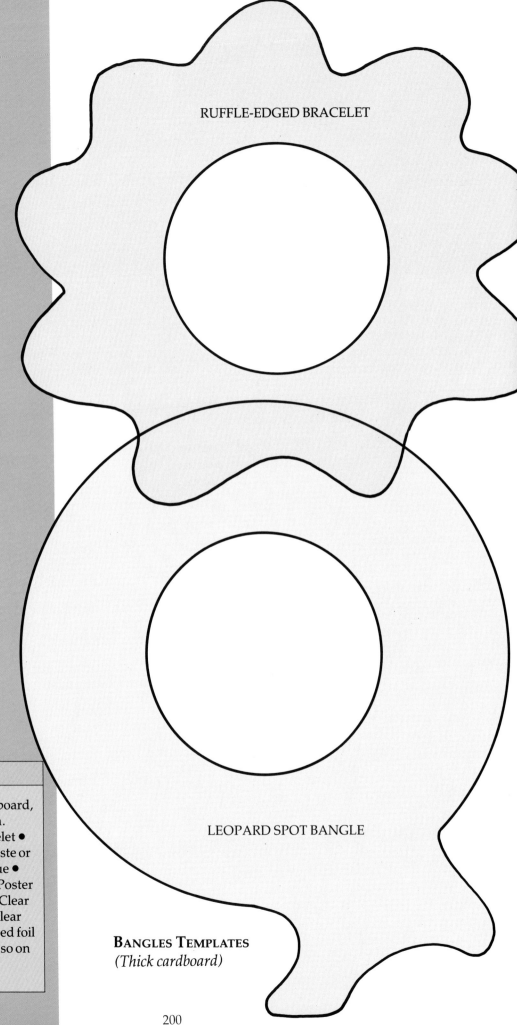

RUFFLE-EDGED BRACELET

LEOPARD SPOT BANGLE

BANGLES TEMPLATES
(Thick cardboard)

YOU WILL NEED

Tracing paper ● Thick cardboard, approximately 8 × 8 in. (20 × 20cm) for each bracelet ● Craft knife ● Wallpaper paste or watered-down white glue ● Paper ● Fine sandpaper ● Poster paints ● Black India ink ● Clear gloss varnish ● Strong, clear glue ● Small pieces of colored foil from sweet wrappers and so on

You could paint your bangle bracelet in one color all over and apply fake gemstones for a glittery, sumptuous effect. You could use small pieces of mirror tile, but be very careful not to cut yourself on the sharp edges! Paper pulp can be added to give extra interest to plain shapes.

Remember that you could also make a bracelet using the same method as the daisy necklace in this section. The modelling-clay shapes will have to be smaller, however, so that the resulting beads are in scale with your hand!

Making your bracelets

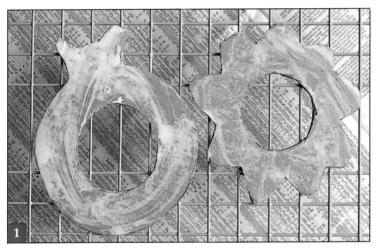

1 Trace the shape you prefer from the patterns in the book and transfer it to the cardboard. Cut around the shape with a craft knife and cut a hand hole in the middle – ask an adult to help you with the cutting. If you are making the ruffle-edged bangle, cut quite precisely around your pattern so that you get a nice smooth edge. Give the bracelet shape a coat of watered-down white glue, and leave it to dry for 4 hours on a wire cake rack.

2 When it is dry, cover the cardboard shape with three layers of pasted paper. Because it is more complicated to cover a curved surface than a straight one, you will have to pay special attention to overlapping the paper smoothly, especially around the inside of the bracelet, where the curve is quite pronounced. Take a little time, and use small, thin pieces of paper. When you have finished papering your bracelet, leave it to dry on a wire cake rack for 24 hours.

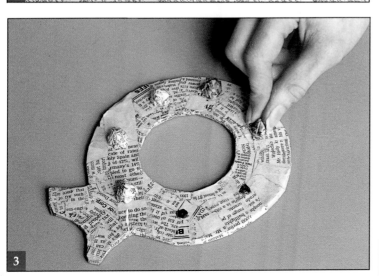

3 Smooth the surface of the bangle lightly with fine sandpaper. At this stage, you can add decorative details in paper pulp if you want to. To make the spots on the leopard bangle, mark six equally spaced dots around the bangle. Take a strip of paper, 1 in. (2.5cm) wide and 4–5 in. (10–12.5cm) long, cover both sides with paste or glue, and roll it up into a little ball between your fingers. Press the pellet on the first of your dots and continue the process until all the dots are covered. Leave the bangle to dry on a wire cake rack for 24 hours.

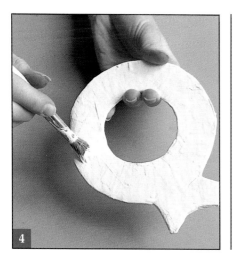

4 When the bangle has dried, sand it lightly and apply two coats of white paint, allowing the first coat to dry before you add the second. The basic shapes can be decorated in many ways.

5 Draw the design on the bangle and start to apply the colors.

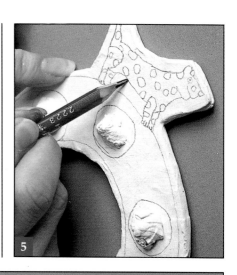

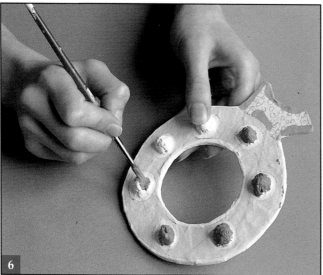

6 The leopard bangle is painted in yellow and dark brown to echo the appearance of the animal's skin.

7 Apply a second layer of paint so that the white paint doesn't show through.

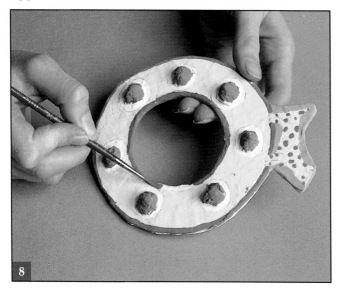

8 Fill in the details, and then, using a fine brush, paint in the black outlines with India ink.

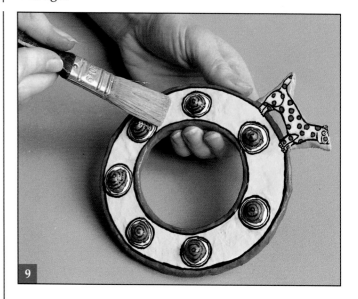

9 Let the bangle dry for 24 hours; then give it two coats of clear gloss varnish.

Ruffle-edged bangle

10 The ruffle-edged bangle is painted in one color. When the paint was dry, it was given a coat of clear gloss varnish and left again to dry. To add the decorations shown in the photograph, spread clear glue on each "petal," and add bits of colored foil from candy wrappers to make interesting patterns. When the glue has dried, decorate the other side of the bangle in the same way. Apply a final coat of clear gloss varnish over the top of the colored foil, and leave the bangle bracelet to dry for 24 hours before you wear it.

Necklace

Exciting jewelry is very simple to make in papier-mâché, and because it is so light, you can wear enormous pieces without being weighed down!

This necklace has been painted in bright, cheerful colors, but you could, of course, paint the beads in a subtler way to achieve a more sophisticated effect. A necklace made entirely of papier-mâché beads is very attractive, but you could alternate colorful wooden, clay, or glass beads with the papier-mâché ones.

The cutout daisy has been added to give a focal point to the necklace. You can use any motif you like.

YOU WILL NEED

Modeling clay, about 1lb. (500g) • Paper • Wallpaper paste or watered-down white glue • Tracing paper • Thin cardboard, approximately 4 × 4 in. (10 × 10cm) • Scissors • Craft knife • Palette-knife • White glue (undiluted) • Masking tape • Fine sandpaper • Poster paints • Black India ink • Clear gloss varnish • Darning needle • Metal eye with ¼ in. (0.5cm) screw shank • Round black elastic, 16 in. (70cm) • Spacer beads (optional)

NECKLACE TEMPLATE *(Thin cardboard)*

HELPFUL HINT . . .

When you are modeling with clay, roll it between the palms of your hands for a few minutes until it becomes soft enough to be molded. If it is a very hot day, on the other hand, and your clay is too soft, put it in the fridge for an hour or so until it has hardened up again.

Making the necklace

1 Roll small pieces of clay into balls, gradually increasing the size from 1 in. (2.5cm) to 1½ in. (4cm) in diameter. Tear small, thin strips of paper, approximately ½ × 2 in. (12mm × 5cm), paste them and start to cover the clay balls. Try to overlap the edges of the strips neatly.

2 When you have covered each ball with five layers, roll them gently between the palms of your hands to smooth the edges. Leave the beads to dry on a wire cake rack for 48 hours.

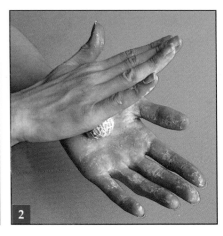

3 Meanwhile, trace the flower motif from the diagram in the book, and transfer it to thin cardboard. Cut around the flower with scissors and paint it with a coat of watered-down white glue to minimize the risk of warping. Let it dry for 2-3 hours, then cover it with three layers of papier-mâché, using small, thin pieces of paper to go around the petals. Leave the flower to dry on a wire cake rack for 24 hours.

4 When the beads are dry enough, carefully cut them in half with a craft knife. **Ask an adult to help you do this.** Leave the opened beads for an hour or so before you remove the clay. This will allow the cut edges to harden slightly and lessen the chances of the papier-mâché tearing when you pull out the clay.

5 Gently prize the clay from the paper casts with the blade of a palette-knife. Let the empty casts dry for 12 hours.

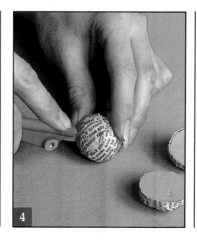

6 When they are dry, smear a little undiluted white glue along the cut edges of each bead and join the halves back together, holding the joins firmly with small pieces of masking tape. Let the glue set slightly, and then, without removing the masking tape, seal the beads with small, thin pieces of papier-mâché. One layer of paper across the joins will be sufficient. Let the beads dry for 24 hours.

7 When the beads and flower motif are dry, smooth their surfaces lightly with fine sandpaper. Give all the pieces two coats of white paint, allowing each coat to dry properly before you apply the next.

8 You are now ready to decorate your necklace. It is up to you how elaborate you make it. This one has been simply decorated, using bright, cheerful colors. First, each bead was painted with a light color. Then, when the paint was dry, a second coat of paint was added. You can use a darker shade of the first color or another color that complements it. Here, the color of the first coat of paint has been allowed to show through the second, and this gives a pleasing mottled effect to the bead.

9 The flower is painted in two colors, chosen to reflect those used for the beads. Again, the petals of the flower have been painted in two shades of the same color, and the lighter shade allowed to show through from underneath. This gives a livelier effect than one flat color, although you may prefer just one shade of pink. Whichever effect you choose, apply two coats of paint, allowing each coat to dry thoroughly before you add the second.

10 When the colors are dry, you can add black ink lines for definition. Swirls of ink have been painted on the beads to emphasize their shape. You will probably have to paint half the bead and let the ink dry for a few minutes before finishing it underneath; otherwise, you might smudge your lines. The daisy has been simply outlined with ink and the shape of its petals defined. Allow the paint to dry for 24 hours.

11 Give each piece of your necklace two coats of clear gloss varnish, allowing the first coat to dry thoroughly before you add the second one. As with the paint, you might find it best to let the beads dry on one side before you varnish the other, to stop them from sticking to your work surface.

12 To assemble the necklace, use a darning needle to make a hole in the top of the daisy motif. Dab a little white glue in the hole and gently screw the metal eye into it. Thread the darning needle with the round elastic and tie a knot in one end. You may need an adult to help you with the next stage. Take a papier-mâché bead and carefully push the needle through the center and out the other side.

13 Pull the elastic through and then, if you are using them, add two spacer beads, followed by another papier-mâché bead. When you have strung half the papier-mâché beads on the elastic, add the daisy motif, which will hang from the elastic by its metal eye, and finish stringing the rest of the beads. Cut the elastic after the last bead, leaving approximately 2 in. (5cm) extra. Tie the two ends of elastic firmly together, and your necklace is ready to wear.

Brooch

This flapping chicken makes a simple, bright brooch, and its bold colors will brighten up your jacket or sweater.

The brooch shape is cut from cardboard and covered with three layers of small papier-mâché strips. The fish shapes in the mobile described later in this book would also make good brooches, as would the flower motif from the necklace.

BROOCH TEMPLATE *(Thick cardboard)*

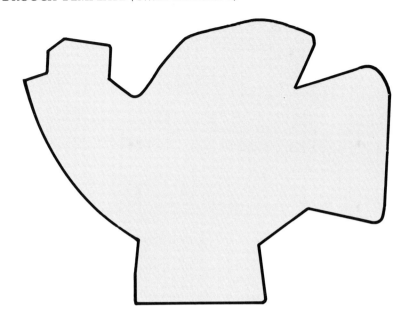

Making the brooch

1 Trace the outline of the chicken from the diagram in the book and transfer it to the thin cardboard. Cut out the chicken with scissors and give it a coat of watered-down PVA adhesive. Lay it on a wire cake rack to dry for 4 hours.

2 Take the cardboard shape and start to cover it with pasted paper. Use small, thin strips of paper, about ½ × 3 in. (12mm × 7.5cm). Try to keep the papier-mâché smooth around the edges so that the brooch will look nicer when it is painted. Apply three layers of papier-mâché, and leave it to dry on a wire cake rack for 24 hours.

YOU WILL NEED

Tracing paper • Thin cardboard, approximately 4 × 5 in. (10 × 12.5cm) • Scissors • Wallpaper paste or watered-down white glue • Paper • Fine sandpaper • Poster paints • Black India ink • Clear gloss varnish • 1 brooch pin • Strong clear glue

3 Smooth the surface of the dry chicken shape with fine sandpaper, and give it two coats of white poster paint, allowing the first coat to dry thoroughly before you add the second.

4 Let the white paint dry thoroughly and draw on the chicken's features in pencil

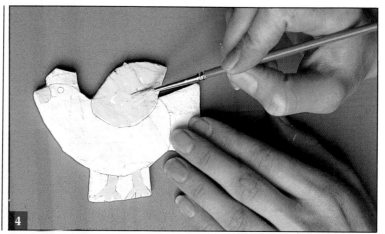

5 Fill in the design with color. You will probably need to use two coats of paint to achieve a good deep color.

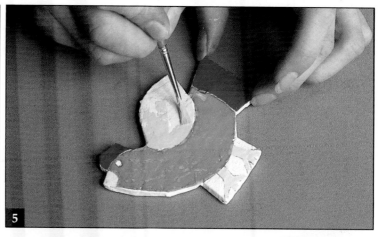

6 Let the paint dry for 4 hours and then paint in the black outline in India ink. Let the brooch dry overnight. Give the brooch two coats of clear gloss varnish, allowing the first coat to dry properly before you add the second. Remember to clean your varnishing brush in soapy water when you have finished.

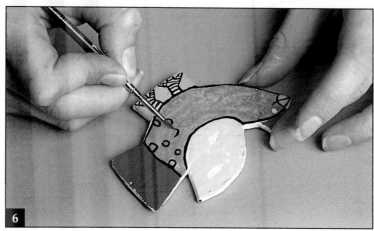

7 Allow the varnish to dry thoroughly; then smear strong, clear glue on the back of the brooch pin.

8 Position it centrally on the back of your brooch, about one-third of the way down, and press it firmly into place. Leave to dry for 24 hours before you wear your brooch.

BOXES

There is a long tradition of making boxes with papier-mâché, especially in the Kashmir region of India, where very solid little pill boxes and trinket chests are produced. They are often beautifully decorated with scenes of horsemen and animals, and flowers are also a favorite motif. The Kashmiri boxes are made from many layers of paper, which are pounded to compress them, and dried in the sun.

The boxes featured in this section are similar in spirit to those of India, but they are made of cardboard which is covered with layers of papier-mâché. The pen and pencil holder, although not strictly a box, has been included in this section because it is used to store or hold objects – the traditional function of boxes. The other boxes are simple in structure, and they close in different ways. One has a fabric hinge along the back, while one has a lid with a "lip" underneath, which fits snugly into the body of the box.

Boxes can, of course, be as large or as small as your want, and they can be made to any design that you please. You could make one with lots of small compartments to store your treasures or perhaps a "double decker," with two levels for letters and stationery. You could also fashion special "packaging" boxes for Christmas presents and birthdays. Not only would they last a long time and be reusable, but you wouldn't need to buy wrapping paper!

Jeweled Box

This little box is decorated very simply and effectively with silver foil and glass "gemstones," and it employs another way of decorating papier-mâché. Sequins would be a good alternative to gemstones, and you could, of course, use different colored foil or perhaps self-adhesive decorative paper to cover the box.

YOU WILL NEED

Thick cardboard, approximately 13 × 11 in. (33 × 28cm) ● Craft knife ● White glue (undiluted) ● Masking tape ● Wallpaper paste or watered-down white glue ● Paper ● Fine sandpaper ● Silver foil ● Strong, clear glue ● Glass "gemstones" in assorted colors

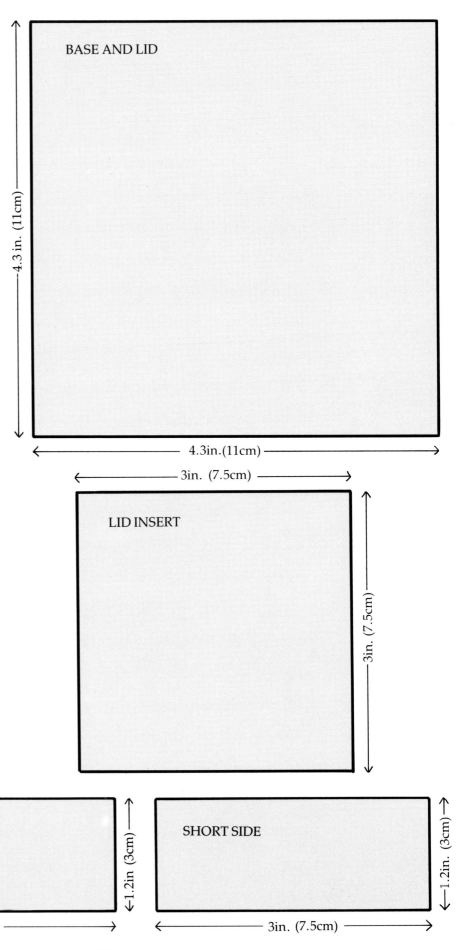

SMALL JEWELED BOX TEMPLATE (*Thick cardboard*)

BASE AND LID

4.3 in. (11cm)

4.3in.(11cm)

3in. (7.5cm)

LID INSERT

3in. (7.5cm)

LONG SIDE

1.2in (3cm)

3½ in. (9cm)

SHORT SIDE

1.2in. (3cm)

3in. (7.5cm)

Making the jeweled box

1 Measure the dimensions from the diagrams opposite and transfer them to the cardboard. Cut them out and form a square out of the wall pieces, holding the pieces together with masking tape. Cover the underside of the walls with white glue and stick the rectangle squarely onto the box base, securing it with masking tape. Then glue the lid insert onto the underside of the lid, holding it in place with tape. Leave everything to dry for a few hours and then give both sections a coat of watered-down PVA. Leave to dry out overnight.

2 Cover both pieces of the box with three layers of papier-mâché. Use strips of paper approximately 1 in. (2.5cm) wide. When you have finished papering, leave the box to dry for 24 hours on a wire cake rack.

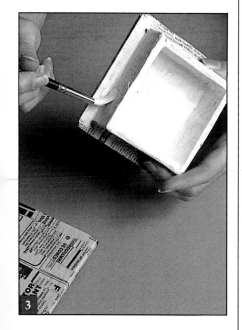

3 Lightly sand the surfaces of your dry box with fine sandpaper and give it one coat of white poster paint. Although you will not see this paint, it will make it easier to apply the foil, which will show up better against white paint than newsprint. Let the paint dry for 3–4 hours.

4 When the paint is dry, the box is ready to be covered in foil. The easiest way is to use long, thin pieces of foil to go around the walls of your box, and large pieces to cover the lid, base, and inside of your box. Cut all the pieces of foil to size before you start gluing it in place. As foil will mold itself to the shape of your box, it is a good idea to fit all the pieces of foil around your box as a trial to make sure they are the right shape and size. Use strong, clear glue to stick the foil down.

5 Once you have glued the foil to your box, leave it to dry for an hour or so before you add the "gemstones." Give some thought to the pattern you want to create, and try a few variations before you glue the stones down permanently. When you have decided on the arrangement, smear a little strong, clear glue on the underside of each stone, and press it firmly onto the box. Let the box dry for 24 hours before you use it.

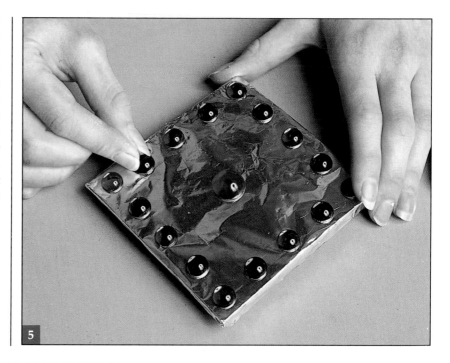

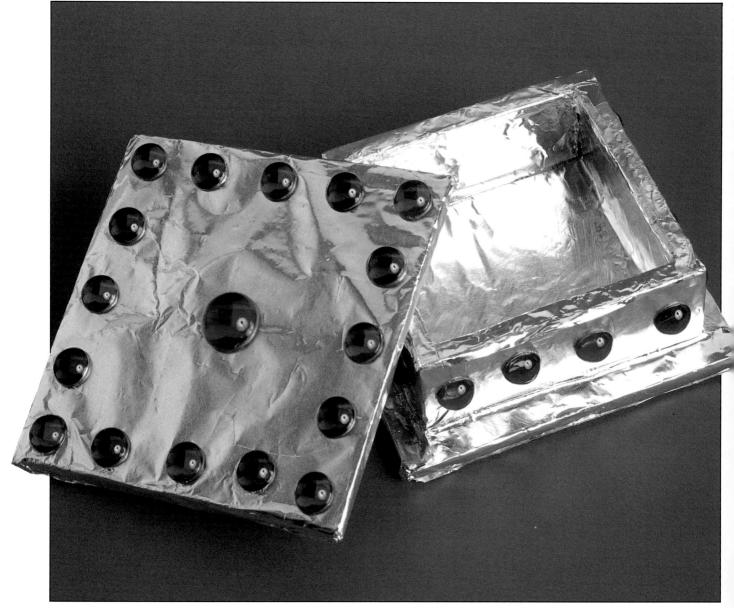

Pen and Pencil Tray

This pen and pencil tray could also be used to hold a multitude of other useful things – scissors, paperclips, and erasers, for example – to help you to keep your desk neat. You could make it to keep sewing things in, or use it as a holder for your paints and brushes. If you made the sides higher, it would hold stationery. Add more compartments or make it bigger to suit your particular hobbies, and decorate it accordingly. You could even make several and build up a stacking system for yourself!

YOU WILL NEED

Thick corrugated cardboard, approximately 17 × 15 in. (43 × 38cm) ● Craft knife ● White glue (undiluted) ● Masking tape ● Wallpaper paste or watered-down white glue ● Paper ● Fine sandpaper ● Poster paints ● Clear gloss varnish

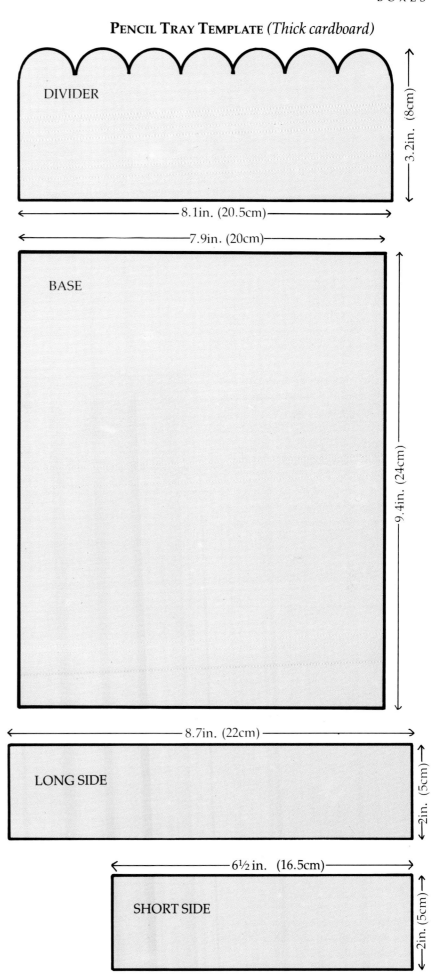

PENCIL TRAY TEMPLATE (*Thick cardboard*)

DIVIDER
3.2in. (8cm)
8.1in. (20.5cm)

BASE
7.9in. (20cm)
9.4in. (24cm)

LONG SIDE
8.7in. (22cm)
2in. (5cm)

SHORT SIDE
6½ in. (16.5cm)
2in. (5cm)

Making the tray

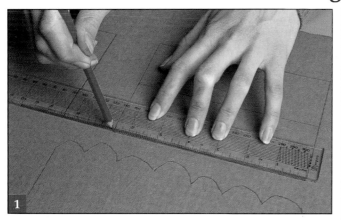

1 Draw the shapes for the base, sides, and divider from the diagram in the book on the cardboard, making sure that you transfer the measurements accurately.

2 Ask an adult to help you cut out the shapes with a craft knife; the blade will be very sharp. Cut the cardboard against a metal ruler.

3 Take the four pieces of cardboard that make up the sides of your pencil tray and glue them together at right angles with undiluted white glue to form a rectangle. Hold the joints securely with masking tape. Smear a little glue along the underside of the joined sides, and place them on the base. When correctly positioned, secure them firmly with masking tape.

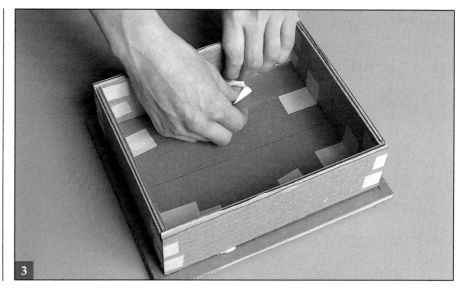

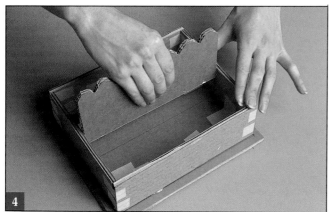

4 Squeeze a line of white glue on the underside and sides of the wavy-edged divider, and position it down the center of the tray. Secure it with masking tape.

5 Now paint the whole tray with watered-down glue, and leave it to dry for 4 hours.

6 When it is dry, cover the tray with three layers of papier-mâché. Use thin, long strips of paper, about 1 × 6 in. (2.5 × 15cm). Take care to push the paper well into the inside corners to give a sharp, smooth look. Use smaller pieces of paper, approximately ½ × 2 in. (12mm × 5cm), to cover the wavy-edged divider, as this will keep it from becoming too lumpy and uneven. Leave the tray to dry for 24 hours.

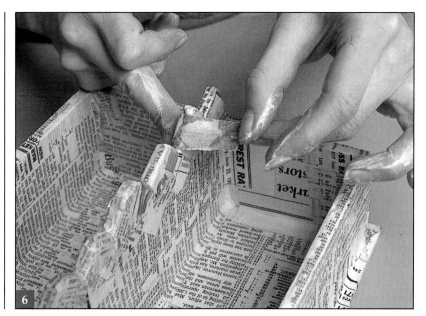

7 When the tray is dry, sand all its surfaces lightly with fine sandpaper and give it two coats of white poster paint, letting each coat dry properly before you add the next. Draw your decoration on the tray. The one illustrated is painted with pictures of the items it might hold – pens, pencils, scissors, and paint-brushes. You might like to use this idea for your tray, or you might want to have an overall design of dots or stripes, executed in contrasting colors, or to write your name in fancy lettering.

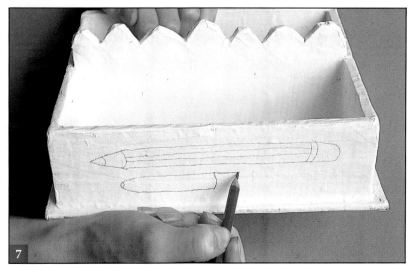

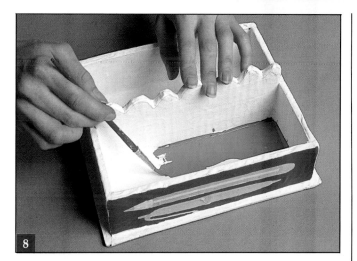

8 When you have drawn in the designs, fill them in with your chosen colors. Remember that the underside of the base will need to be decorated, too.

9 You will need to apply two coats of paint to achieve a good, dense covering, but do not add the second coat until the first one is completely dry. When you have finished painting your tray, outline your design with black India ink.

10 Let your tray dry overnight, and then give it two coats of clear gloss varnish, allowing the first to dry before applying the second. Remember to clean your brush thoroughly with soap and water when you have finished varnishing.

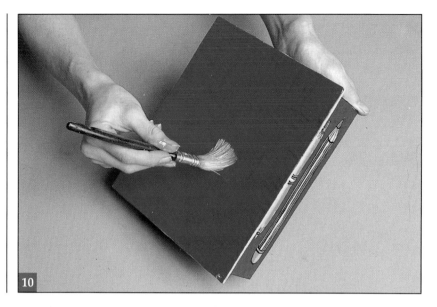

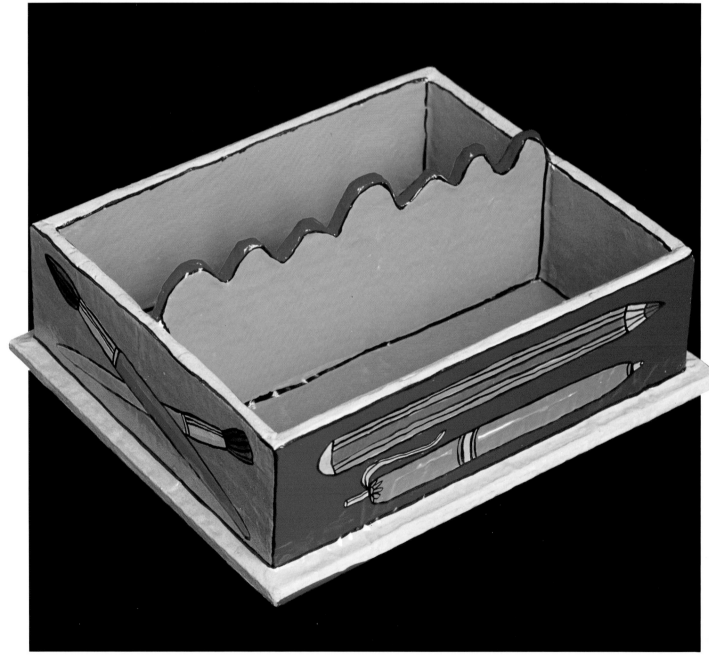

Hinged Box

This box, which closes with a hinged lid, is decorated with a technique known as découpage. *This involves collecting interesting scraps from such sources as magazines, newspapers, and greeting cards. The cutout scraps are stuck onto objects as a decoration and varnished in place.*

This box has been decorated with black and white engravings that were photocopied from an old encyclopedia, but almost anything that you like would be suitable.

YOU WILL NEED

Thick cardboard, approximately 16 × 14 in. (40 × 36cm) ● Craft knife ● White glue (undiluted) ● Masking tape ● Wallpaper paste or watered-down white glue ● Paper ● Fine sandpaper ● Cotton ribbon, 1 in. (2.5cm) wide and 4 in. (10cm) long ● An assortment of scraps cut from newspapers, magazines, greeting cards, wallpaper books, etc. ● Clear gloss varnish

---

HINGED BOX TEMPLATE *(Thick cardboard)*

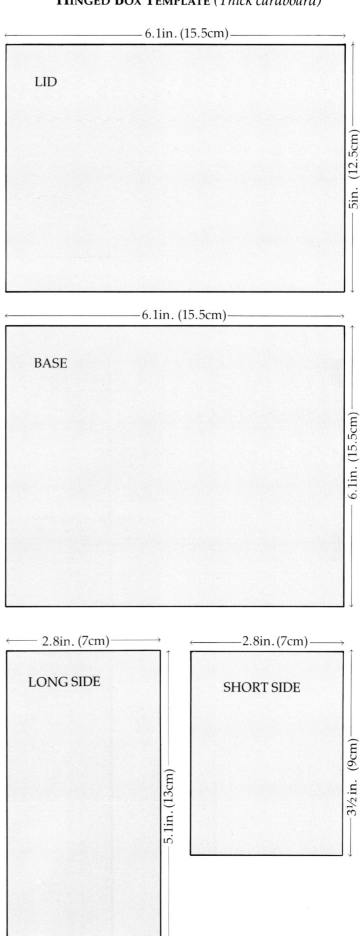

6.1in. (15.5cm)

LID

5in. (12.5cm)

6.1in. (15.5cm)

BASE

6.1in. (15.5cm)

2.8in. (7cm)

LONG SIDE

5.1in. (13cm)

2.8in. (7cm)

SHORT SIDE

3½in. (9cm)

Making the hinged box

1 Accurately transfer the measurements for each piece of the box from the diagram in the book onto the cardboard. Ask an adult to cut each piece out for you with a craft knife and metal ruler. Take the pieces of cardboard that make up the sides and smear the edges with white glue. Join them at right angles and secure the joins firmly with masking tape.

2 Give all the pieces of the box a coat of watered-down white glue and leave them to dry for 4 hours on a wire cake rack. Cover the underside of the joined side section with white glue, and place it squarely on the base. Tape the joins together with masking tape. Leave the glue to set for an hour or so, and then cover the box pieces with three layers of papier-mâché. Let them dry overnight on a wire cake rack.

3 When the papier-mâché is dry, smooth it down with fine sandpaper. Fold the piece of ribbon in two along its length and coat half its width with undiluted glue. Press the glued ribbon along the back top edge of the box body. Put glue on the other half of the ribbon, and press it onto the box lid. You will probably have to support the lid on a pile of magazines or one or two books while the glue dries. Cover the edges of the ribbon hinge with two layers of papier-mâché, avoiding the crease along the center, and let it rest on its support for 24 hours.

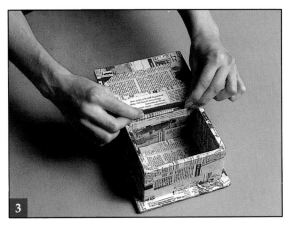

4 When it is completely dry, lightly sand the extra papier-mâché around the hinge and give the whole box two coats of white poster paint.

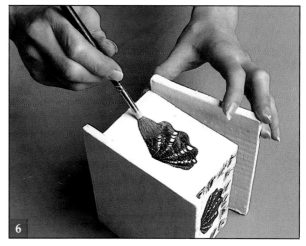

5 Let the paint dry thoroughly, and then start to arrange your cutout scraps, trying out several designs before you glue them down. Use a little undiluted glue to stick the scraps to the box, and leave them to dry for a few hours in a warm place.

6 If you are leaving some of the box surface white, use watered-down glue, but not too much, as a varnish, since clear gloss varnish tends to look slightly yellow on top of white. Otherwise, use clear gloss varnish. Whichever you use, give your box two coats, allowing the first coat to dry thoroughly before you apply the second. Leave your box to dry for 24 hours before you use it.

Heart-shaped Box

This box is decorated with pieces of colored foil from candy wrappers. It is fairly simple to make in spite of its shape and can be used to contain a variety of small objects including jewelry, money, and candy. It would make a pretty gift, especially for Valentine's Day!

HEART-SHAPED BOX TEMPLATE *(Thick and thin cardboard)*

BASE AND LID *(Thick cardboard)*

Guide line for box wall

1.2 in.

12.6 in. (32cm)

BOX SIDE *(Thin cardboard)*

(3cm)

LID INSERT *(Thick cardboard)*

Making the heart-shaped box

1 Trace the shapes from the diagram in the book, transferring the outlines for the base and top to the thick cardboard and the outline for the side to the thin cardboard. You should lay it to the card so that the corrugations run vertically, which will make it easier to curve the shape as it is being stuck down. Cut out all the box pieces. **Ask an adult to help you as you will need to use a craft knife, and its blade will be very sharp.** Take the length of thin card that will form the box side. Bend it gently along its length at every corrugation so that it curves easily as you stick it along the guideline on the base. Coat the underside edge of the box wall with white glue, and glue it carefully along the guideline. Secure it every 1–1½ in. (2.5–4cm) with masking tape.

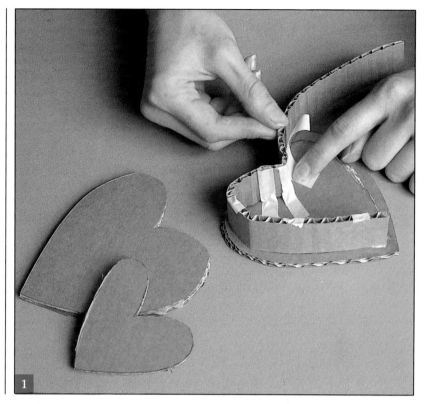

2 Place the lid insert centrally on the back of the lid. Draw a pencil line around it, and cover the back of the lid insert with strong, clear glue. Press it back on the lid inside the pencil line. Leave the lid and the base to dry for an hour or so, and then give both pieces a coat of watered-down white glue. Leave both pieces to dry for about 4 hours in a warm place.

3 Cover both pieces with two layers of papier-mâché and leave them to dry for 24 hours on a wire cake rack.

4 When both parts of the box are dry, smooth them lightly with fine sandpaper and give them two coats of white poster paint, allowing the first coat to dry before you add the second.

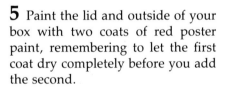

5 Paint the lid and outside of your box with two coats of red poster paint, remembering to let the first coat dry completely before you add the second.

6 Give the inside of the box two coats of paint; the inside of the box illustrated here has been painted yellow, but you can use any color you like. Let the paint dry thoroughly, and then varnish the box with one layer of clear gloss varnish. Leave the box to dry for 24 hours.

7 When the varnish is dry, you can begin to glue the decorations on. Cut out pieces of foil and use strong, clear glue to glue them to the varnished surface of the box. Your pattern can be as flamboyant or as simple as you like. You may want to line the box with foil, too.

8 Allow the box to dry overnight and then varnish carefully over the foil additions, taking care not to lift them off with your brush. Let the first layer of varnish dry thoroughly and then add another. As always, clean your brush in soap and water when you have finished with it.

FRAMES

Simple frames for pictures and photographs are quite easy to make and can be decorated in a variety of ways. They can be made especially for a particular picture or photograph, with the frame echoing or embellishing the image, or they can be more general in appearance so they look good with a variety of pictures.

You can use all kinds of things to decorate your frame – broken pieces of pottery arranged to create a mosaic effect, brightly colored foil from candy wrappers, sequins, buttons, shells, glass "gemstones," and so on. The frames featured here are finished off with gilt disks and pebbles found on the seashore. You can choose the idea that most appeals, or you might like to combine two or three ideas in one frame.

The frames described here close in different ways. The heart-shaped frame is sealed, and its contents are permanently enclosed.

The frame with the heart-shaped opening is hinged on one side and fastens with a bow.

Heart-shaped Frame

This is a permanently sealed frame, so you will have to decide carefully what to put inside it before you make it. It is decorated with two different sizes of gilt coins – the kind that are sewn on scarves and costumes – and they give it a sumptuous appearance. There is no need to buy things to decorate it, though; old brass and gilt buttons would look just as good, especially if you used several different sizes and colors.

YOU WILL NEED

Thick cardboard, approximately 12 × 10 in. (30 × 25cm) • Tracing paper • Thin cardboard, approximately 12 × 10 in. (30 × 25cm) • Craft knife • Wallpaper paste or watered-down white glue • Paper • Fine sandpaper • Acetate, 4½ × 3½ in. (11 × 8cm) • Strong, clear glue • Masking tape • 2 paper brads • Poster paints • Clear gloss varnish • Gilt disks, old brass buttons, sequins, pebbles, etc. • Thin cord, 8 in. (20cm) long

The picture of the sun has been enclosed in the frame because it is so cheerful, but you might like to put in a special photograph instead. Because you won't be able to remove it once the frame is sealed, you might prefer to make a color photocopy of your picture and keep the original. The contents of the frame are protected by a small piece of acetate, which keeps dust and dirt from settling on the picture.

Making the heart-shaped frame

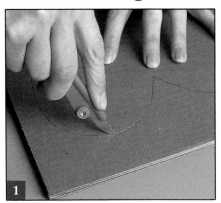

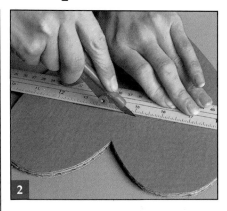

1 Draw a large heart on the thick cardboard. Make it about 10 in. (25cm) long from top to bottom and 8 in. (20cm) across at its widest point. Trace the shape of this heart exactly on the tracing paper and transfer it to the thinner card. Ask an adult to help you cut around the heart shapes with a craft knife.

2 Use a ruler to draw a rectangle approximately 4 in. (10cm) wide and 2¾ in. (7cm) high in the center of the thick cardboard. This will be the opening of your frame. Ask an adult to help you with the craft knife. Coat both pieces of cardboard with watered-down glue and dry them for 4 hours on a wire cake rack.

3 When they are dry, start to cover both pieces of frame with papier-mâché. Use pieces of torn paper about 1 in. (2.5cm) wide, and when you paper around the opening in the front of the frame, try to keep the papier-mâché nice and smooth. Cover the frame pieces with three layers of papier-mâché and leave them to dry for 24 hours.

227

HEART-SHAPED FRAME TEMPLATE (*Thick cardboard*)

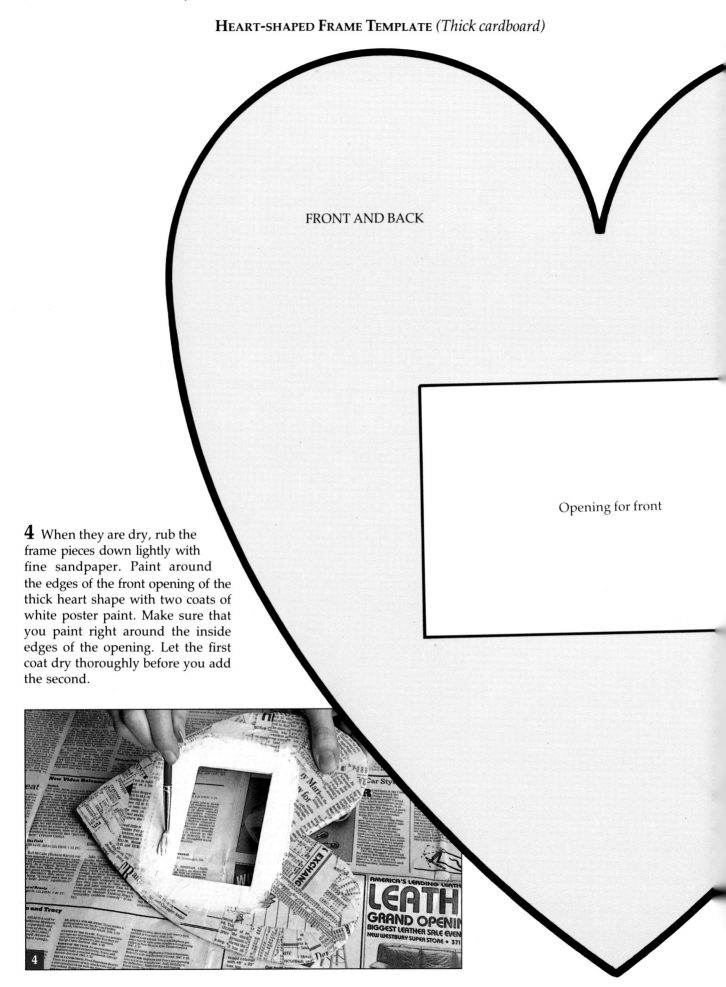

FRONT AND BACK

Opening for front

4 When they are dry, rub the frame pieces down lightly with fine sandpaper. Paint around the edges of the front opening of the thick heart shape with two coats of white poster paint. Make sure that you paint right around the inside edges of the opening. Let the first coat dry thoroughly before you add the second.

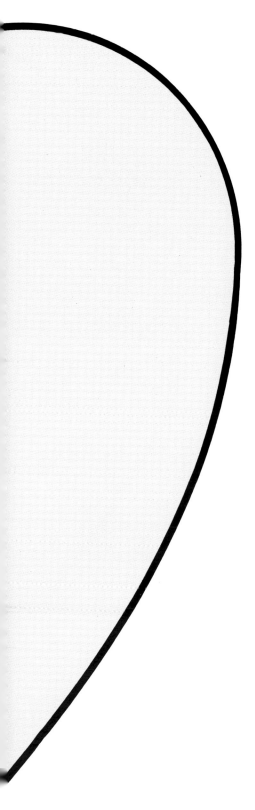

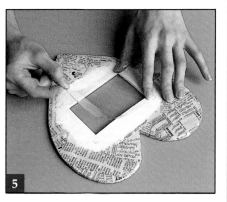

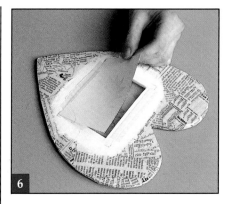

5 When the white paint is dry, lay the piece of acetate over the opening in front of the frame. It doesn't matter which side you put the acetate on, but remember that this is now the **inside** of the frame. Mark around the edges of the piece of acetate with pencil. Smear the edges with a little strong, clear glue and lay the acetate back down within your pencil marks, securing it in place with masking tape.

6 Take your picture and lay it on top of the acetate, again on the inside of the frame. Make sure that the picture is the right way around and that you can see it through the acetate from the front of the frame! When you are sure that your picture is straight and looks right from the front, tape it in place with masking tape.

7 Ask an adult to help you make two small cuts in the thin heart shape with a craft knife. Make each one 3 in. (7.5cm) from the top of the heart and 2 in. (5cm) from the center on each side. These cuts are for the paper brads, which will act as picture hangers. Push a brad into each cut. You are going to glue the thin heart to the back of the thick heart, so make sure that the heads of the brads are outside the thin heart and that their shanks are on the inside.

It is easy to check if you have put the brads in the right way around – the side with the shanks emerging from it should fit neatly over the inside of the thick heart shape. If it doesn't, remove the brads from the thin heart, and push them through from the other side. Open the brads out and tape over the flattened shanks with masking tape. Then cover the tape with a layer of papiermâché, and leave the heart to dry overnight.

Joining the front and back

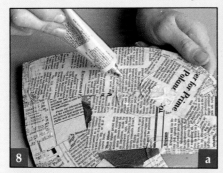

8 When the thin heart is dry, spread glue on its inside surface (a). Carefully glue the thin heart to the back of the thick heart (b) and hold the hearts together with masking tape (c).

9 Let the glue set for an hour or so, and then seal the edges of your frame with small strips of papier-mâché. Try to avoid getting splashes of glue on the acetate, especially if you are using watered-down white glue. Apply two layers of paper and leave the frame to dry for 24 hours.

10 When it is dry, rub down the frame with fine sandpaper, and paint it with two coats of white emulsion, taking special care around the heads of the brads. Allow the first coat of paint to dry thoroughly before you add the second. Let the frame dry for 2 hours.

11 Now give the frame two coats of poster paint. Leave it to dry thoroughly for 24 hours, and then paint it with 2 coats of clear gloss varnish, allowing the first coat to dry before you apply the second. Remember to clean your varnishing brush in soap and water when you have finished.

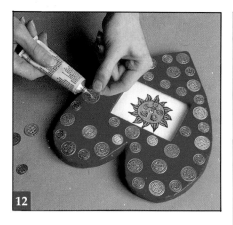

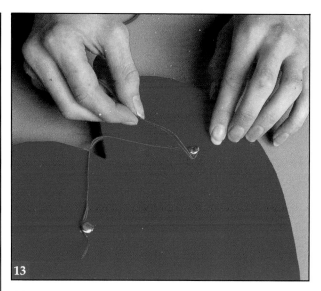

12 When the second coat of varnish is dry, take the decorations you have chosen, for example, gilt disks, and arrange them in a pattern. When you are satisfied with the design, coat the backs with strong, clear glue and press them firmly to the frame.

13 Allow the frame to dry thoroughly and tie the cord around the heads of the brads on the back. The frame is now ready to hang up.

Square Frame with Heart-shaped Opening

This frame has a distinctive heart-shaped opening. It has a hinge and is fastened at one side with a thin ribbon bow.

Although this design would be good to give as a Valentine's Day present, you could make the opening any shape you like and make the frame as large or as small as you please. You could even have several openings in the frame and keep a variety of pictures or photographs in it.

YOU WILL NEED

Thick cardboard, approximately 14 × 14 in. (36 × 36cm) ● Craft knife ● White glue ● Masking tape ● Wallpaper paste or watered down white glue ● Paper ● Fine sandpaper ● Cotton tape, 1 in. (2.5cm) wide and 8 in. (20cm) long ● Narrow cotton ribbon, 8 in. (20cm) long ● Strong, clear glue ● Poster paints ● Black India ink ● Clear gloss varnish ● Black felt, approximately 7 × 7 in. (17.5 × 17.5cm) ● Scissors

SQUARE FRAME WITH HEART-SHAPED OPENING TEMPLATE (*Thick cardboard*)

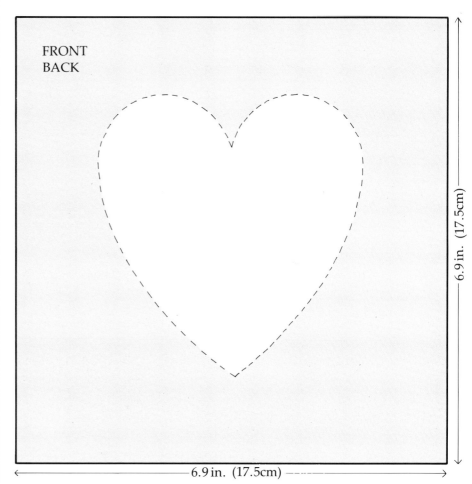

FRONT
BACK

6.9 in. (17.5cm)

6.9 in. (17.5cm)

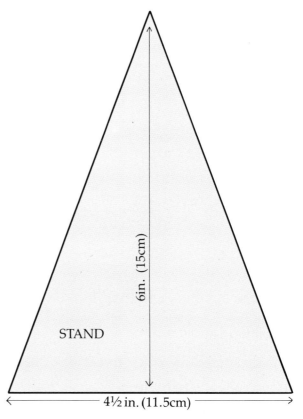

6 in. (15cm)

STAND

4½ in. (11.5cm)

Making your frame

1 Mark out the measurements for the front and back of the frame on the cardboard. Be sure to transfer the measurements correctly. Ask an adult to help you cut out the frame and stand pieces with a craft knife, because the knife will be very sharp.

2 Measure a point halfway along the top and bottom edges of the back. Use a ruler to join these two points with a pencil line. Coat one long edge of the stand with white glue and place it along the line on the back. Hold the stand firmly in position with masking tape and leave the glue to set for a couple of hours.

3 Give the frame pieces a coat of watered-down white glue, and let them dry on a wire cake rack for 4 hours. Cover all the pieces with three layers of papier-mâché. Make sure that you do not knock the stand out of position. Let the frame pieces dry on a wire cake rack overnight.

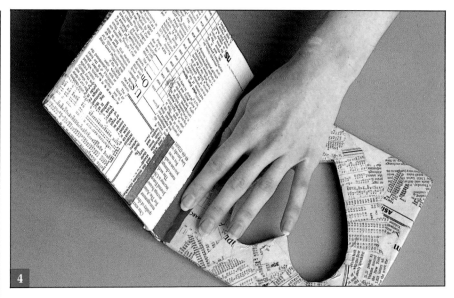

4 Lightly rub down the dry pieces with fine sandpaper. Fold the tape you are going to use as the hinge in two lengthwise and spread undiluted white glue on half of it. Glue the tape to the right-hand edge of the inside of the front of the frame. Smear glue on the other half of the tape, and stick it to the edge of the back. While the tape is drying, prop the frame slightly open so that it doesn't stick to itself.

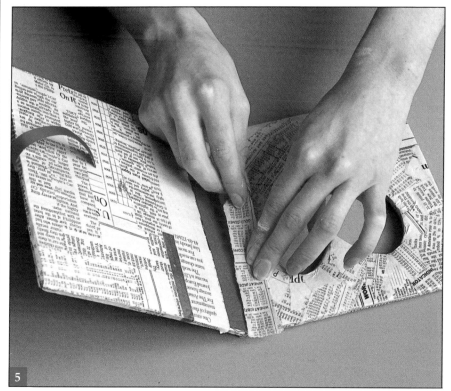

5 When the tape is dry, open the frame. Measure two points, one halfway down the inside of the left-hand side of the front of the frame and one halfway down the right-hand side of the back. Mark these points and glue half the length of narrow ribbon to each with strong clear glue. Hold the lengths of ribbon in place with masking tape. Cover the edges of the hinge tape and the ribbon with two layers of papier-mâché. Leave the frame to dry for 24 hours.

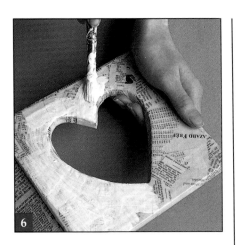

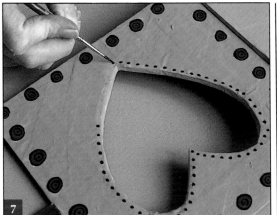

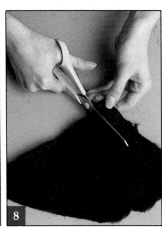

6 Lightly sand the extra papier-mâché, and give your frame two coats of white poster paint, allowing the first coat to dry before you add the second. Leave to dry.

7 Draw a design on the frame with pencil and fill it in with color. Don't forget to paint the back, too. Allow the paint to dry for 4 hours and then add detail to your design with black Indian ink. Let the frame dry overnight and then apply two coats of clear gloss varnish.

8 Take the piece of black felt and use scissors to cut it to the same size as the back. Smear it with undiluted PVA adhesive, and stick it carefully to the back so that it covers the edge of the thin ribbon. Let your frame dry overnight before you use it.

FESTIVALS

This section contains some projects that you can make in papier-mâché to celebrate the year's special occasions. The Christmas decorations are jolly and bright, and they can be made in several sizes. You could make a robin several times the size of the template, for example, and hang it from ribbon as a decorative plaque. Other shapes would make good wall decorations, too – bells and holly leaves, for example. Rather than painting the tree decorations, you might like to cover the shapes in gold, silver, or colored foil and add a touch of sparkle to your tree!

Easter bunnies and Easter eggs can be made over molded clay, which is removed when the paper has dried. You could leave an opening under the bunny and fill him with candy for an extra surprise, as is done in several countries. It would be fun to use the same method to make an Easter chicken to accompany him. Easter eggs can be made in several sizes, and if you plan to make a lot, you could even buy special metal egg molds – which are really for making chocolate eggs – and use them for your papier-mâché if you don't want to make them from clay. If you do use a metal mold, remember to grease it with petroleum jelly first.

Christmas Cutouts

These cheerful cutouts can be used as decorations to brighten up your Christmas tree, but you needn't stop there – they will lend a festive atmosphere to any part of the house and will look especially decorative displayed at a window.

Once you've painted and varnished them, you might like to add sequins or fake gemstones to give them an extra sparkle!

YOU WILL NEED

Tracing paper ● Thin cardboard, approximately 10 × 10½ in. (25 × 26cm) for each decoration ● Scissors ● Wallpaper paste or watered-down white glue ● Paper ● Fine sandpaper ● Poster paints ● Black India ink ● Clear gloss varnish ● Darning needle ● White glue (undiluted) ● Metal screw eyes, one for each decoration ● Thin colored cord, 8 in. (20 cm) for each decoration

CHRISTMAS DECORATIONS TEMPLATES (*Thin cardboard*)

BOW

STAR

ROBIN

236

Making the cutouts

1 Trace the decoration shapes from the book and transfer them to your thin cardboard. Cut out the cardboard shapes with scissors. Give each decoration a coat of watered-down white glue and let them dry on a wire cake rack for about 4 hours. When they have dried somewhat, cover your pieces with pasted paper, using strips about ½ in. (12mm) wide and 2 in. (5cm) long.

2 Cover each decoration with three layers of papier-mâché and place them on a wire cake rack to dry for 24 hours.

3 When the shapes are dry, smooth them lightly with fine sandpaper and give them two layers of white poster paint; allow the first coat to dry properly before you add the second. Let the paint dry for 4 hours.

4 Draw in the features or patterns on your decorations with pencil and start to apply the colour with your paints. You will probably have to use two coats of paint to cover the white paint properly.

5 Leave the paint to dry for 4 hours, then use black India ink to outline and emphasize the details. Let the decorations dry overnight.

6 When they are thoroughly dry, paint your decorations with two coats of clear gloss varnish, allowing the first coat to dry properly before you add the second. Remember, as always, to clean your brush in soap and water when you have finished with it.

7 When the varnish is dry, ask an adult to help you to make a hole in the top of each decoration with a darning needle. Dab a little white glue into each hole, and screw the metal eyes into each hole as far as they will go. Be careful to keep the screws straight so that they do not emerge from the sides of your decorations. Leave the decorations to dry for a few hours until the glue has set. All that remains to do is to tie the thin cord to the top of each metal eye. Tie a loop in the top of each length of cord once it is fastened to a decoration and hang it from your tree.

Easter Eggs

These Easter eggs are made in the same way as the bunny, using modeling clay as a mold. A piece of thin cardboard is used to make a lip to hold the two halves together.

If you are giving the eggs as Easter gifts, you might like to put little presents – charms or candy, for example – inside them as a surprise.

Making the Easter eggs

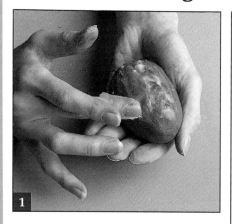

1 Break the clay into lumps that are about the size you want each finished egg to be. Roll each piece of clay between the palms of your hands to soften it, and then work it into an egg shape. Add or take away clay as necessary, and finally cover the eggs with petroleum jelly.

2 When you are satisfied with your egg shapes, tear up your paper into pieces about the size of postage stamps and start to cover the eggs. Try to mold the paper smoothly over the clay. Cover each egg shape with eight layers of papier-mâché, and leave them to dry in a warm place for 2–3 days.

3 When the papier-mâché feels dry, ask an adult to cut each egg into two equal halves. It is probably easiest to make the first cut with a craft knife through the papier-mâché to the clay all the way around each egg, and then to use a kitchen knife with a serrated blade – a bread knife, for example – to saw through the clay.

YOU WILL NEED

Modeling clay, 4–8 oz. (150–250g) for small to medium eggs; 1 lb. (500g) for large eggs • Petroleum jelly • Paper • Wallpaper paste or watered-down white glue • Craft knife • Serrated knife • Palette-knife • Fine sandpaper • Poster paints • Black India ink • Clear gloss varnish • Pieces of thin white cardboard • Clear, strong glue

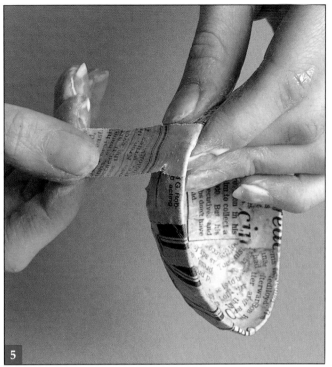

5 Bind all around the cut edges of each empty shell with small strips of paper, approximately ½ × 2 in. (12mm × 5cm). One layer of binding strips will be sufficient. Let the shells dry overnight on a wire cake rack.

4 Leave the opened eggs to dry on a wire cake rack for an hour or so, and then, using the blade of a thin palette-knife, gently prize the clay away from the walls of each papier-mâché egg.

6 Lightly sand the shells inside and out, and give each one two coats of white poster paint, allowing the first coat to dry thoroughly before you add the second.

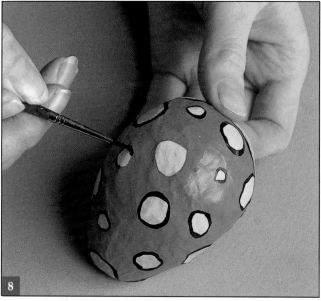

7 Draw designs on the outside of the painted shells and start to fill them in with color. You will probably need two coats of paint to achieve a good, deep color.

8 Allow the paint to dry for 4 hours, and outline your designs with black India ink. Let the eggs dry overnight.

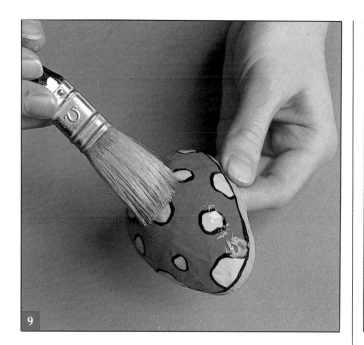

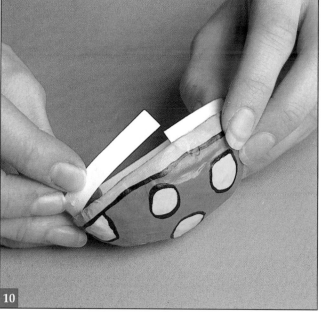

9 Give each eggshell two coats of clear gloss varnish. Paint the varnish on one side at a time, and let it dry completely before you do the other. Allow the first coat to dry on each side of your eggs before you add the second.

10 Measure around the inside edge of one half of each egg. Cut a piece of thin white cardboard this length and about ½ in. (12mm) wide. Coat the card with clear, strong glue down one long edge, and spread a thin line of the same glue around the inside edge of one eggshell. Let the glue on both surfaces dry slightly and press the card around the inside of the eggshell. Make sure the ends join neatly.

11 Let your eggs dry thoroughly before you fit them together.

Easter Bunny

This Easter bunny was made on molded clay, cut in half and then joined back together with small strips of paper. Before it was joined together, it was painted white inside because it is open at the bottom so that candy can be stuffed inside it. In some countries, candy is sealed inside papier-mâché toys, which are smashed open by the children who receive them. But it would be a shame to break this bunny after you've decorated him!

Making your bunny

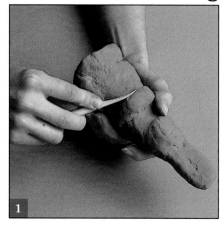

1 Soften the clay between the palms of your hands and shape it into a block about 8 in. (20cm) long, 3 in. (7.5cm) deep and 3 in. (7.5cm) wide. Use pottery modeling tools or something similar to mold the bunny shape. The bunny illustrated has a very simple design, but you could make it more ornate if you wanted to.

2 Smear a little petroleum jelly over the clay, thinly and evenly.

3 When you are happy with the shape of your clay bunny, tear up the paper into pieces the size of postage stamps and start to cover him. Take care to mold the paper smoothly, and try to make sure that each layer covers the bunny completely before you begin to apply the next, so that he doesn't have any thin patches. It is a good idea to use two colors of paper if you can so that you can alternate the colors with each layer. Cover the bunny with eight layers of papier-mâché, and put him in a warm place to dry for 2–3 days.

YOU WILL NEED

Modeling clay, 1 lb. (500g) ● Pottery modeling tools or similar ● Paper ● Petroleum jelly ● Wallpaper paste or watered-down white glue ● Craft knife ● Serrated knife ● Palette-knife ● Masking tape ● Scissors ● White glue (undiluted) ● Fine sandpaper ● Poster paints ● Black India ink ● Clear gloss varnish

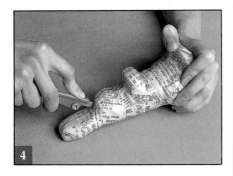

4 When the papier-mâché feels dry, draw a line down the center of the front and back of your bunny, making sure that it divides him into two equal halves. Ask an adult to cut the bunny in half for you by making an initial cut with a craft knife and then slicing through him with a serrated knife such as a bread knife.

5 Place the opened halves of the bunny on a wire cake rack. Let the edges harden for an hour or so, and then use the blade of a thin palette-knife to push the clay gently away from the edges of the paper casts. Lever the clay out of each half, and leave the papier-mâché to dry overnight on a wire cake rack.

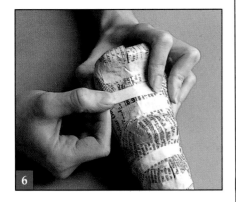

6 Tape the two halves of your bunny together, making sure that they join accurately, and draw an oval on the underside.

7 Untape the halves and cut out the oval with a pair of scissors. Pick any small traces of clay off the inside of each cast, and paint the insides with two coats of white poster paint, allowing the first to dry completely before you add the second.

8 When the painted insides are dry, smear the cut edges of each half bunny with undiluted white glue. Join the two halves together, making sure that they fit closely, and anchor them firmly with masking tape. Allow the bunny to dry on a wire cake rack for 2 hours. Cover the join with two layers of small paper strips, and bind the edges of the oval in the underside of the bunny. Let him dry overnight on a wire cake rack.

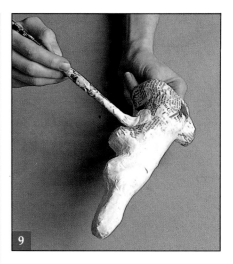

9 Lightly sand down the surface of your bunny with fine sandpaper, and give him two coats of white paint, allowing the first to dry before you add the second. Remember to paint over the paper strips on the inside edge of the oval opening.

Decorating your bunny

10 When the white paint has dried, draw the design on your bunny with pencil and start to fill it in with color. You will probably need to use two coats to achieve a good, deep color. Let the paint dry for 4 hours, and then define the design with black India ink. Let the bunny dry overnight.

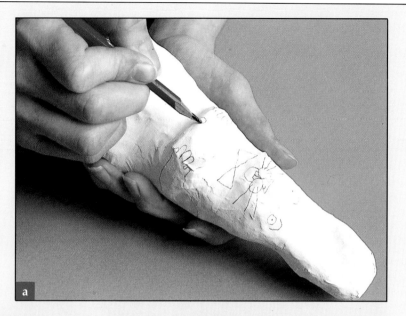

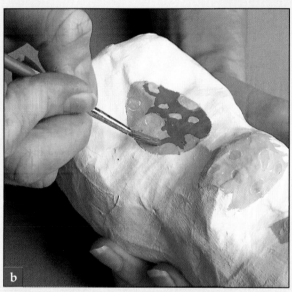

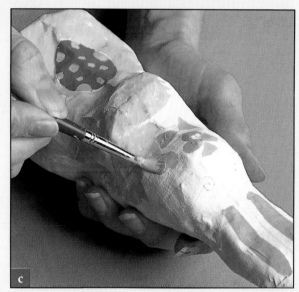

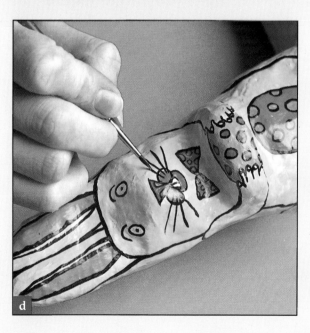

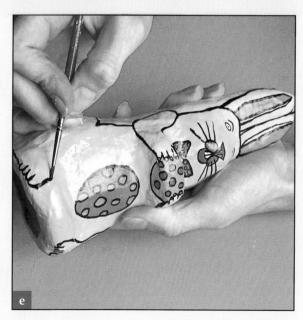

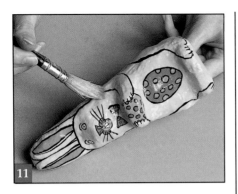

11 Give your bunny two coats of clear gloss varnish, allowing the first to dry thoroughly before you add the second. Remember to clean your brushes in soap and water when you have finished. When your bunny is dry, you can fill him with candy.

HELPFUL HINT . . .

If you make a mistake when you are adding details in black India ink, let the ink dry and then paint over it with a little white paint paint. When the paint is dry, you can easily cover up the mistake with the original background colour and draw in the black line again.

TOYS

Papier-mâché is ideal for making toys because it is so versatile – you can make almost anything you like with a little thought and planning! This section shows you how to make masks, a mobile, a jointed toy elephant, and puppets. You can let your imagination run wild to create fabulous masks and puppets. You could make characters from your favorite books and games or perform a masked play with your friends. Put on a puppet show at your school or club – you could ask your friends to write short plays and sketches and perform them with puppets.

Dolls are also fun to make in papier-mâché. You can make them over molded clay, in the same way as the Easter bunny in the Festivals section. Make them rigid, all in one piece so that they cannot be repositioned, or make the arms and legs separately and join the limbs to the body with round elastic.

Jointed Elephant

This handsome elephant has movable legs, ears, and tail. His body is made from thick cardboard, while thinner cardboard is used for his limbs, ears, and tail, which are held in place with paper brads. These brads, which can be bought from stationery shops, act as pivots and allow you to reposition the elephant's limbs.

YOU WILL NEED

Tracing paper • Thick cardboard • Thin cardboard • Scissors • Craft knife • Wallpaper paste or watered-down white glue • Paper • Fine sandpaper • 7 paper brads • Masking tape • Poster paints • Black India ink • Clear gloss varnish.

JOINTED ELEPHANT TEMPLATES *(Thick and thin cardboard)*

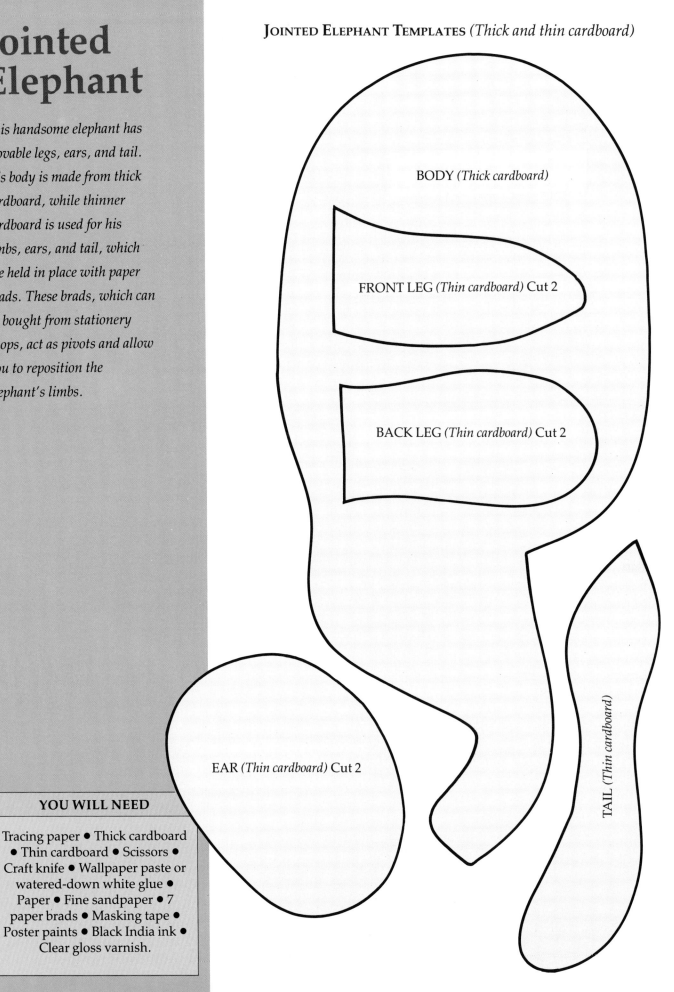

BODY *(Thick cardboard)*

FRONT LEG *(Thin cardboard)* Cut 2

BACK LEG *(Thin cardboard)* Cut 2

EAR *(Thin cardboard)* Cut 2

TAIL *(Thin cardboard)*

Making your elephant

1 Trace the elephant pieces from the pattern and transfer them to the cardboard. Remember to use thick cardboard for the body and thinner card for the movable parts. Cut around each piece with scissors. Ask an adult to help you cut the thicker cardboard, as the craft knife will be very sharp.

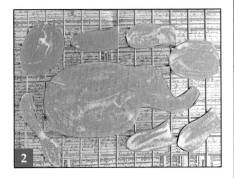

2 When all the pieces are cut, give them a coat of watered-down white glue to help prevent them from warping when papier-mâché is added. Leave the pieces to dry on a wire cake rack for 4 hours.

3 Tear your paper into thin, short strips, ½ in. (12mm) wide and 3 in. (7.5cm) long, and cover the pieces of cardboard with three coats of papier-mâché. Leave the shapes to dry overnight on a wire cake rack.

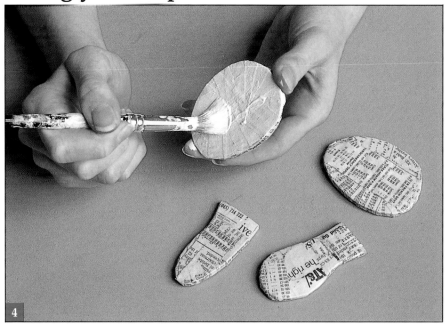

4 When the shapes are dry, smooth them with fine sandpaper and give each one two coats of white poster paint, taking care to let the paint dry thoroughly between each coat.

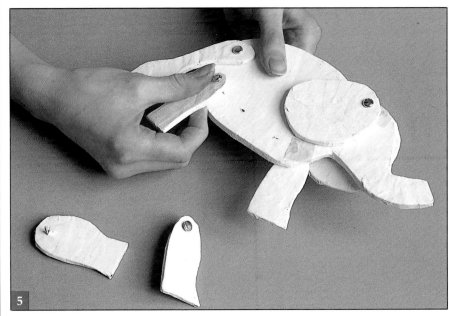

5 The legs, ears, and tail are joined to the body with brads. So that the shanks of each brad can pass through the cardboard, you have to make a small incision toward the top center of each movable piece. Ask an adult to help you with this, because you need a craft knife, which will have a very sharp blade. Pass the shanks of a brad through each little hole. Ask an adult to help you make similar incisions in the elephant's body for the brads to pass through. You need to make seven holes, one for each of the legs and ears and one for the tail. Remember that some pins have to go from the front to the back of the body and some from the back to the front, but you can make room for them by moving each piece to one side once it has been fixed.

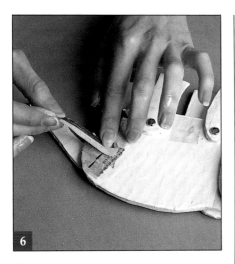

6 When all the brads are in place, cover the opened-out shanks of each one with masking tape. Cover the tape with strips of papier-mâché, and leave your elephant to dry over-night, propped upright if possible.

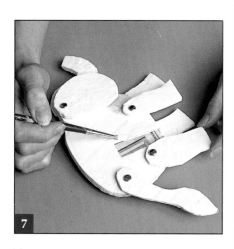

7 When the papier-mâché is dry, carefully sand it down and give the elephant two coats of white paint, allowing the first to dry completely before you add the second.

HELPFUL HINT . . .
Leave your papier-mâché objects in the driest place in the house – but away from direct heat.

Painting your elephant

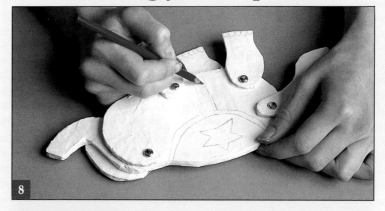

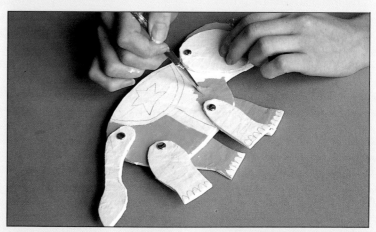

8 Draw in the elephant's toenails, tusks, eye, and blanket, and paint the elephant with poster paints. You will have to move his limbs carefully so that you can paint him properly, and you will probably have to come back to the underside of his ears and legs several times because you won't be able to paint everything all at once. Remember that your elephant has two sides, so paint both sides the same.

9 When you have finished painting the colors in, let your elephant dry for 4 hours, and then add the outlines and details in black India ink. Leave your elephant to dry overnight, and then give him two coats of clear gloss varnish, allowing the first coat to dry thoroughly before you add the second. When you are varnishing around his limbs, take care that they don't stick to his body. When you have finished varnishing, clean your brush thoroughly with soap and water.

Face Mask

One of the simplest ways of making a mask is to use a balloon as a mold. The resulting paper shape, when cut in half lengthwise, will make a lovely oval, which can be painted just as it is or used as a base on which to build facial features with cardboard, chicken wire, and so on.

The mask illustrated here is decorated very simply with eyebrows, a pair of glasses, and a nose cut from cardboard and stuck on. Ears are added, and fake fur is used to create sideburns and bushy eyebrows.

YOU WILL NEED

Tape measure • 1 balloon • Petroleum jelly • Paper • Wallpaper paste or watered-down white glue • String • Scissors • Small pieces of thin cardboard • Strong, clear glue • Masking tape • Fine sandpaper • Poster paints • Black India ink • Clear gloss varnish • Fake fur, cotton balls, string, yarn, pieces of felt and similar for hair, beard, and moustache • Darning needle • Round elastic • Tracing paper

1 Measure your face from about 1 in. (2.5cm) above the start of your hairline to 1 in. (2.5cm) below the end of your chin. Blow up the balloon – you may have to ask an adult to help you – until it is slightly longer than your hairline-to-chin measurement. Tie the end of the balloon tightly to stop it from going down, and grease it with a thin layer of petroleum jelly. This will allow the dried paper cast to be removed from the balloon and will also mean that if the balloon does go down slightly, your papier-mâché won't shrivel with it! Place the balloon in an empty bowl.

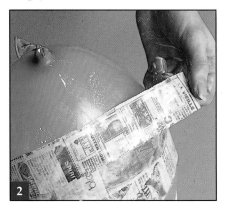

2 Tear up your paper into strips about 1 in. (2.5cm) wide and 10 in. (25cm) long and start to cover the balloon.

3 You will find it easier to remember whether you have finished a layer or not if you use two different colors of paper, alternating colors with each layer. When you have covered your balloon with eight layers of papier-mâché, tie a length of string to the end and suspend it in a warm place to dry. It will probably take 3 days to dry out completely.

4 When the papier-mâché feels dry, burst the balloon by sticking a pin through the paper; pull the deflated balloon out of the cast by the string. Draw a line lengthwise around the center of the papier-mâché. Ask an adult to help you cut around the line with sharp scissors.

5 Take one of the paper halves. This will be your mask. You will need to mark the openings for your mouth and eyes on the inside of the mask. The easiest way to do this is to put some lipstick on your mouth, fit the balloon half over your face and, when it feels comfortably in place, "kiss" the inside. The lipstick will leave a clear mark that you can use as a guide for the mouth hole, which can be cut into any shape you want.

7 Now position the glasses, nose, and eyebrow pieces on your mask. Anchor them in place with strong, clear glue, and secure them firmly with masking-tape while they dry.

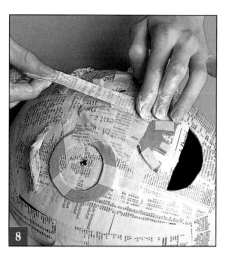

8 When the glue is dry, cover the cardboard additions with two layers of papier-mâché. Bind the cut edges of the mouth hole, and, if you have made them large, the edges of the eye holes. Also bind the outside edge of the mask, and leave it to dry for 24 hours.

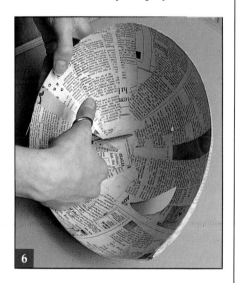

6 To find out where the eye holes should go, measure a straight line from the top of your lower lip to the top of your nose, between your eyes. Mark this on the inside of your mask, taking the lipstick mark as your starting point. Now measure from the top of your nose to the center of each eye. Mark these measurements on the inside of your mask. Make a small hole at each center eye mark, and if you have measured correctly, you will be able to see through. Make the eye holes as big or small as you want, but **do not** try to enlarge the holes while you are holding the mask against your face.

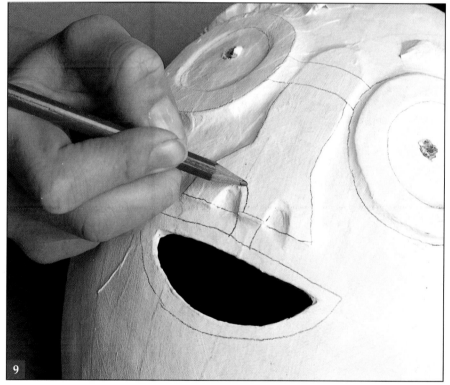

9 Smooth the surface of the dry mask with fine sandpaper and give it two coats of white paint, both inside and out, allowing the first coat to dry before you add the second. When the paint is dry, draw the design onto the mask.

Painting the mask

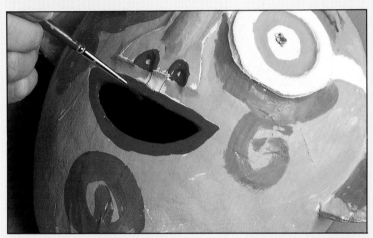

10 Draw a design on the mask in pencil, and start to fill it in with color. You can make your decoration lifelike, or you could let your imagination run riot and create a strange and fabulous face.

11 Leave the paint to dry for 4 hours. Outline your design with black India ink and let the mask dry overnight. Paint the mask with two coats of clear gloss varnish, allowing the first coat to dry properly before you add the second. Remember to clean your varnishing brush in soap and water when you have finished.

12 When the varnish is dry, you can stick on hair and beards and moustaches. Lots of materials can be used for this, including fake fur, cotton, string, yarn and felt. Use strong, clear glue; then leave your mask to dry overnight. All that remains to do is to attach the elastic to your mask so that you can wear it. Place the mask against your face, and ask a friend to mark a spot just above your ear on each side of the mask.

13 Ask an adult to help you make a hole at each spot with a darning needle. Enlarge the holes until they are wide enough for the elastic to pass through. Thread the elastic through the mask from the inside to the outside and tie a knot in the end. Push the elastic through the other hole from the outside to the inside, pull it tight and tie a knot. Cut off the excess elastic; your mask is now ready to wear.

Monster Mask

This monster mask is made, like the other mask, over a balloon mold, but the resulting paper shape is cut around rather than lengthwise, so that it fits over the head like a helmet. The monster has strange, golden protruberances growing from the top of its head and seven eyes, but the effect is humorous rather than scary. The golden spikes have been made with empty cones from rolls of yarn, but if you can't find these, you can make your own cones from rolled-up cardboard just as easily.

YOU WILL NEED

Tape measure • 1 balloon • Petroleum jelly • Paper • Wallpaper paste or watered-down white glue • String • Scissors • Craft knife • White glue (undiluted) • 6 empty knitting wool cones or cones made of thin cardboard • Masking tape • Fine sandpaper • Poster paints • Black India ink • Nontoxic gold craft paint • Clear gloss varnish

Making a monster mask

1 Measure around your head, holding the tape measure over the mid-point of your ears. Blow up the balloon – you may need an adult to help you at this point – until it is slightly larger at its widest point than your head measurement. Tie the balloon tightly, and grease it with a thin coat of petroleum jelly. Stand the balloon in an empty bowl.

2 Tear the paper into strips about 1 in. (2.5cm) wide and 10 in. (25cm) long and cover the balloon with eight layers of papier-mâché. If possible, use two colors of paper alternately so that you can see when you have finished each layer. Tie a length of string to the end, and hang your balloon to dry in a warm place for 2–3 days.

3 When the papier-mâché is dry, burst the balloon by sticking a pin through it; pull the deflated balloon through the bottom of the cast. Measure a line from the center of the top of your head down the front of your face to the bridge of your nose. This line should be long enough to reach to about 1 in. (2.5cm) below your eyes. Transfer this measurement to the front of your balloon. Make a pencil mark at the center of the balloon, measure straight down until you have the same length as the distance from the top of your head to your nose and make a mark. Repeat this measurement from the same central point several times, working your way around the balloon until you have a row of dots. Join this line of dots and ask an adult to help you cut along it with sharp scissors.

4 Place the paper "helmet" over your head, and hold the paper between finger and thumb, fingers outside and thumbs directly in front of each eye – your fingers will show you where. Ask someone to help you mark the spots on the outside of the mask. Draw in two eye shapes, and ask an adult to help you cut out these shapes with a craft knife. **Never** try to make the eye holes while you are wearing the mask. Arrange the cones, about 4 in. (10cm) high, on the crown of your mask. When you are happy with their position, draw around the base of each. Coat the underside of each cone with white glue, and place them back in position inside the drawn lines. Hold them firmly in position with masking tape. Let the glue set for a couple of hours, then cover the cones with two layers of papier-mâché. Make sure that you cover the joins well.

5 Bind around the cutout eyes and around the edge of the mask with small pieces of papier-mâché. Stand it on a wire cake rack to dry for 24 hours. When the mask is dry, sand it lightly with fine sandpaper and give it two coats of white paint, allowing the first coat to dry thoroughly before you add the second.

Painting the mask

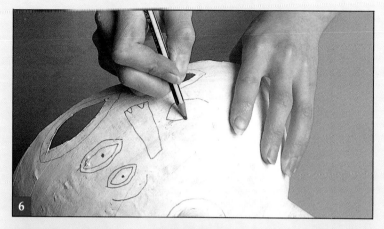

6 When the paint has dried, draw a design on the mask and start to fill it in with color. The mask illustrated here has been decorated very simply, but it would lend itself perfectly to more flamboyant designs. When you have finished painting your mask, let it dry for 4 hours and then outline your design with black India ink. Paint the spikes with gold craft paint, and leave the mask to dry for 24 hours.

7 The mask should now be painted with two coats of clear gloss varnish, but be careful not to varnish over the gold paint on the spikes. Let the first coat of varnish dry before adding the second coat, and remember to clean your brushes in warm soapy water when you have finished.

Mobile

The fish in this mobile float gracefully around a central shell, suspended from a crossbar. Mobiles have long been favorites with children and babies, and are often hung over their cribs and beds to amuse them. Your mobile need not feature fish – brightly colored geometric shapes would be very effective – and, of course, you'll probably want to be more adventurous than this. The main thing to remember when you choose your shapes is that they will have to hang in the same mobile and should look as if they belong together!

YOU WILL NEED

Tracing paper • Thin cardboard, approximately 10 × 10 in. (25 × 25cm) • Thick cardboard, approximately 10 × 10 in. (25 × 25cm) • Scissors or craft knife • Wallpaper paste or watered-down white glue • Paper • White glue (undiluted) • Masking tape • Fine sandpaper • Poster paints • Black India ink • Clear gloss varnish • 6 metal screw eyes • Darning needle • Thin cord or strong thread, approximately 45 in. (112cm)

MOBILE TEMPLATES *(Thick and thin cardboard)*

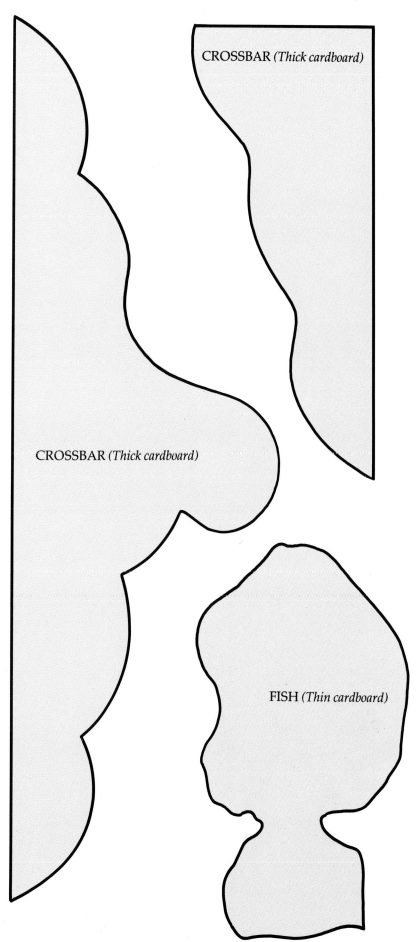

CROSSBAR *(Thick cardboard)*

CROSSBAR *(Thick cardboard)*

FISH *(Thin cardboard)*

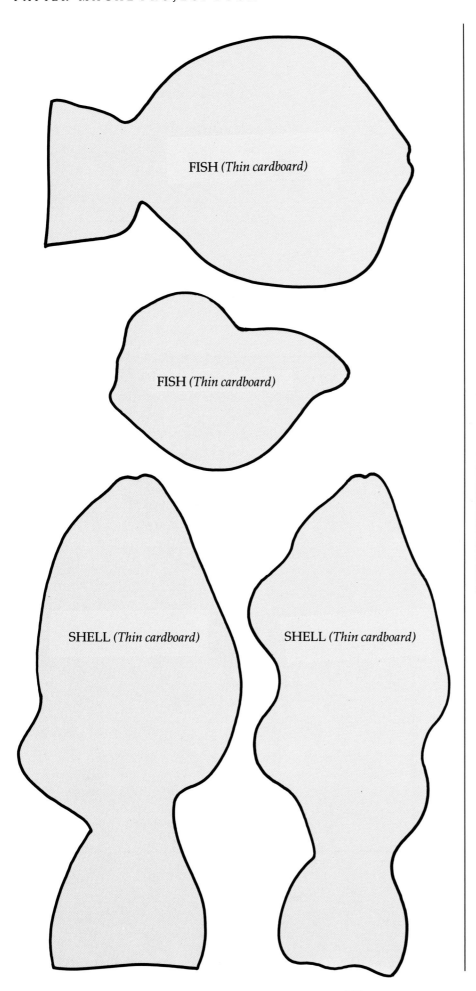

FISH *(Thin cardboard)*

FISH *(Thin cardboard)*

SHELL *(Thin cardboard)*

SHELL *(Thin cardboard)*

As mobiles are suspended in the air, you might like to make one that features flying things – planes, insects, or hot air balloons, for example – or things that appear in the sky, such as stars or planets. Perhaps these are flying fish in the mobile illustrated here!

Making the mobile

1 Trace the fish and shell motifs from the book, and transfer the shapes to the thin cardboard. Trace the crossbar shapes, and transfer them to the thick cardboard. Cut out the shapes using scissors or a craft knife, but ask an adult to help you if you use a craft knife because the blade will be very sharp. Coat each cutout piece with watered-down white glue, and leave them to dry on a wire cake rack for 4 hours.

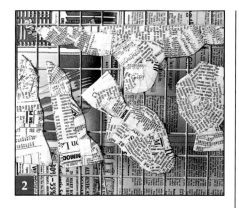

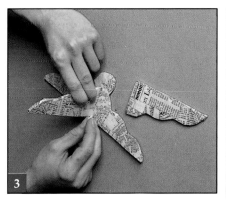

2 Tear your paper into strips about ½ in. (12mm) wide and 3 in. (7.5cm) long and start to cover your cardboard shapes. Three layers of papier-mâché will be sufficient for each fish. Try to keep the edges neat and smooth, as the finished effect will be more pleasing. Cover the shell motif and sections of crossbar in the same way and leave your papered shapes to dry on a wire cake rack for 24 hours.

3 Take the dry cross-pieces and join them at right angles as shown in the photograph. Coat the edges of both short pieces with undiluted white glue, and, after positioning them on the main piece of the crossbar, anchor them firmly with masking tape. When the glue has set for a couple of hours, paper over the joints with thin strips of papier-mâché. Let the crossbar dry for 24 hours.

4 When all the pieces are dry, rub them down lightly with fine sandpaper and give each piece two coats of white poster paint; remember to allow the first coat to dry before you add the second one.

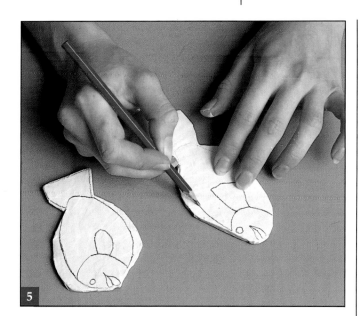

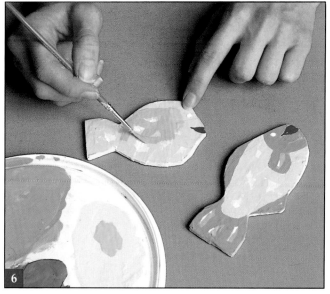

5 Draw the features on the white fish shapes with pencil. Try to give each fish a different expression so that your mobile looks interesting. Draw the spiral on the shell shape, and don't forget the shell on the top of the crossbar!

6 Paint the mobile pieces. If you want to create a mottled effect, paint your pieces with progressively darker shades of the same color, allowing each coat of paint to dry thoroughly before adding the next one.

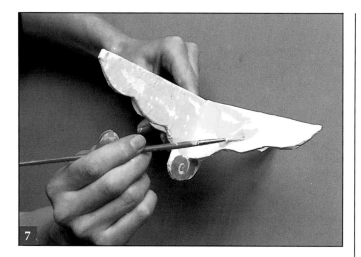

7 The crossbar is decorated simply in varying shades of yellow and orange. As with the fish and shell, a light color is used for the first coat of paint, and this is followed by two or three slightly darker shades, finishing with orange. Let the paint dry, and then add the black outlines in India ink.

8 Varnish the finished pieces of mobile before you join them together. Give each piece two coats of varnish, allowing plenty of drying time between each coat. Remember to clean your varnishing brush with soap and water when you have finished.

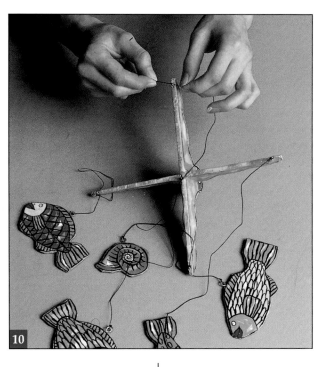

9 The fish and the shell are suspended from the crossbar by thin cord or strong thread, which is fastened to a metal eye screwed into the center of each piece. To attach the metal eye, use a darning needle to make a hole in the back of each fish, halfway along its length. Make a hole in the same way in the top of the shell. Dab a little undiluted white glue into each hole, and carefully screw a metal hook into each piece. Don't turn the screw too roughly or it may go in crooked and emerge from the side of your fish!

10 Make holes about ½ in. (12mm) from the end of each arm of the crossbar. Dab them with glue and screw in the metal eyes carefully. Attach an eye in the center of the crossbar from which the shell will be suspended. Make sure that you place it squarely, so that the shell looks balanced. Finally, screw an eye into the top of the crossbar, in the center back of the shell. The fish and shell are now ready to be suspended from the crossbar. A mobile looks best if its decorations are hung at varying heights, so that it is possible to see each piece clearly. With this in mind, cut four pieces of cord or thread of different lengths. Tie the end of each thread to the metal eyes in the back of each fish. Use a double knot to make sure that the thread is firmly held. Tie the other end of each piece of thread to a different arm of the crossbar.

11 Your mobile is now ready to hang up. Decide how far you want it to drop from the ceiling or from wherever it is going to hang, and cut an appropriate length of thread. If you are making this mobile for a very young child or baby, make sure that it is hung high enough to be out of their reach so that they can't pull it down and chew it! Tie one end of the thread to the eye in the top of the crossbar, and make a loop in the other end. The mobile can now be hung in place. It will look very effective if it is hung where there is a slight breeze to move it, and you may even like to tie bells to the threads so that it tinkles as it moves!

HELPFUL HINT . . .

When you have finished varnishing, always clean your brush carefully in soapy water. If you use the sort of varnish that requires turpentine to clean your brushes, ask an adult to help you.

Puppets

Puppets are great fun, and there are several ways of making them. Here is one of the simplest and most effective methods.

This sort of puppet is known as a glove puppet because it fits over your hand like a glove. You use your middle finger to hold its head upright and your other fingers to operate its hands.

Each puppet's head is modeled in clay, which is removed when the papier-mâché has dried and been cut open. The two halves of the head are then glued back together again. Features can be added in paper pulp after the clay is removed.

YOU WILL NEED

Modeling clay, about 1 lb. (500g) for each puppet head ● Pottery modeling tools or similar ● Paper ● Wallpaper paste or watered-down white glue ● Craft knife ● Serrated knife ● Palette-knife ● White glue (undiluted) ● Masking tape ● Fine sandpaper ● Poster paints ● Black India ink ● Clear gloss varnish ● Felt, 2 pieces approximately 9 × 9 in. (23 × 23cm) for each puppet, and scraps for hands ● Tracing paper ● Plastic-headed pins ● Needle and thread ● Decorative braid, approximately 28 in. (70cm) for each puppet ● Strong, clear glue

TUNIC FOR PUPPETS TEMPLATES

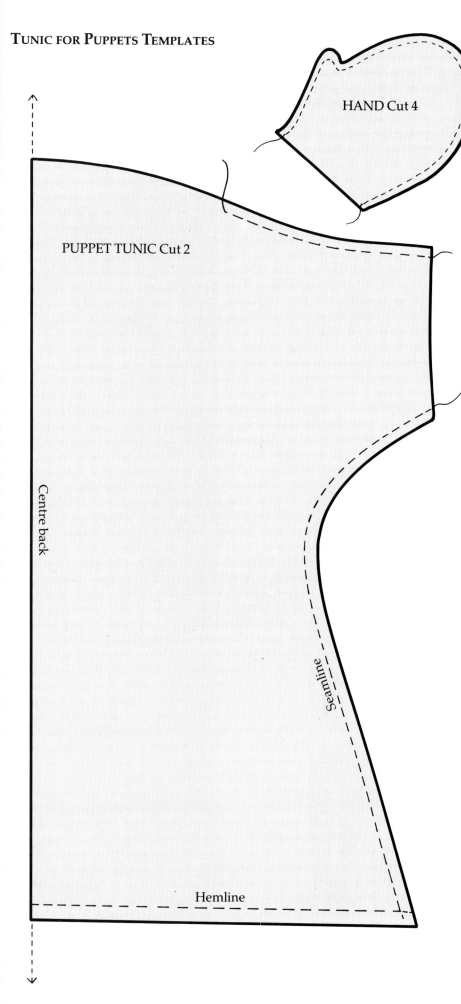

HAND Cut 4

PUPPET TUNIC Cut 2

Centre back

Seamline

Hemline

Your puppet's face should be painted in a striking way. If the character it portrays is usually happy, paint it with a beaming, jolly face. If it is a king or queen, try to make it look regal and haughty. Remember, the puppet may be 10 ft. (3m) or more away from your audience, if you use it in a puppet theater and the puppet performs inside it, so it is important that its features are bold and bright.

The puppets featured here are wearing dresses made from brightly colored felt with sparkly gold braid trims. However, it would be easy to make really ornate costumes for them, using sumptuous fabrics, sequins, fake fur, and so on. The costumes can be sewn by hand or machine, so don't despair if you haven't got a sewing machine!

Making the puppets

1 Form your clay into a large lump about 4 in. (10cm) high and 3 in. (7.5cm) thick. When you are satisfied with the size of the lump, start modeling your puppet's features. You should aim to make the mold as accurate as you can, with the eyes, nose, and mouth where you want them. At this stage, however, there is no need to make the details too fine, because they will be lost when the clay is covered with paper. Remember that you can accentuate features with paper pulp when the clay has been removed.

2 Use small pieces of paper about the size of postage stamps, because you will be able to mold the papier-mâché more closely and smoothly around the clay. When you have covered the clay with eight layers of papier-mâché, lay the head on a wire tray to dry. It may take 3–4 days to dry completely, but if you leave it in a warm place, it should be ready to cut open after 48 hours. When the head feels dry on the outside, it should be cut open and the clay removed. Ask an adult to do the cutting for you, as it will be necessary to use a craft knife to make the first cut. Cut all the way around the head, making sure that the cutting line is straight. It doesn't matter whether the head is divided down the nose or through the ears, as long as the line is straight. When the initial cut has been made, it is a good idea to finish the cutting with a serrated knife – a bread knife, for example – as it will be awkward to cut through the depth of clay with a short-bladed knife.

3 Once the head is cut in two, let the inside edges of the paper casts dry for 1–2 hours; otherwise, they might be a bit too fragile to remove the clay. When the edges have become firmer, take a small palette-knife and gently insert it between the clay and the edge of the paper "cast." Push the clay away from the sides of the paper, taking care not to split the papier-mâché, and gradually pull out chunks of clay. When you have removed all the clay, leave the paper halves to dry for 2–3 hours.

4 The two halves of the head now need joining together again. Spread a little undiluted white glue along the edges of each half and fit them together, holding them firmly in place with masking tape. Make sure that the edges fit neatly, or an ugly join line will be visible. Let the glue set for an hour, and then cover the join with small strips of paper. Two layers will be enough to seal it quite tightly.

5 Now is the time to add more pronounced features to your puppet with small amounts of paper pulp if you want to. You will need long, thin strips of paper. Dip them in the wallpaper paste or watered-down white glue, and scrunch them up between your fingers, squeezing out the excess glue. Arrange the pulp directly on the puppet's head. You can be quite flamboyant here, and give your king a luxuriant beard or your queen an ornate crown. Let the pulp additions dry for 24 hours. When they have dried, cover them with a layer of small paper strips and leave them to dry.

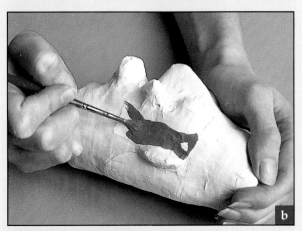

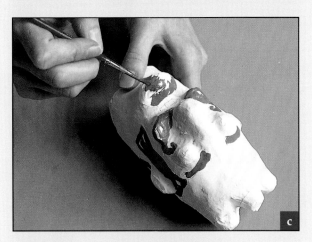

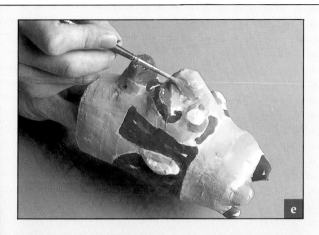

7 Leave the head to dry overnight and give it two coats of clear gloss varnish, allowing the first coat to dry thoroughly before you add the second. Clean your brush in soap and water when you have finished.

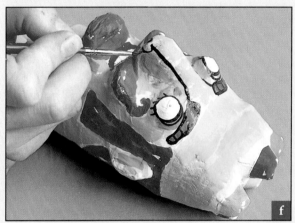

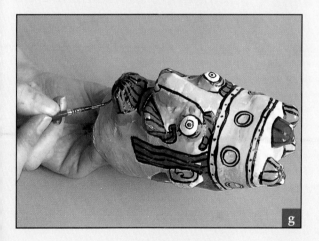

6 When the head is dry, sand it lightly and give it two coats of white paint. Draw in your puppet's features with pencil and start to fill them in with color. Leave the paint to dry for 4 hours, then define the face with black India ink.

Painting the puppet's head

Dressing your puppet

8 To make the clothes, trace the tunic patterns from the diagrams in the book onto tracing paper. Cut out the tracing-paper pattern and pin it to two thicknesses of felt. Cut carefully around the pattern and unpin it. Pin the two sides of the tunic together, right sides facing. If you have an adult to help you, the tunics can be sewn together by machine, or you can do it by hand. The seam should be about ¼ in. (5mm) from the edges of the material. Leave the neck open. Measure around your puppet's neck, and sew the neck opening of the tunic so that the head fits in snugly.

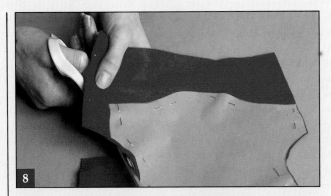

9 Trace the hand pattern from the diagrams onto tracing paper. Cut out the paper pattern and pin it to your felt. Cut out four hand shapes and sew two together for each hand, again leaving ¼ in. (5mm) for each seam. These seams will remain on the outside of the hands, so make your stitches as neat as you can. Cut lengths of gold braid to go around the sleeves and hem of the puppet's tunic. Sew the braid in place with running stitch.

10 Place one stitched hand just inside each sleeve. Pin through the sleeve to keep the hand in place and sew it to the sleeve with small running stitches. Stitch the excess sleeve material together and take out the pins.

11 Slip your puppet's head into its tunic to check that it fits. Smear a little strong, clear glue onto the puppet's neck and the inside neck openings of the tunic. Let the glue dry slightly, and then position the puppet's neck inside its tunic. Let the glue dry, and cover the join with gold braid. Stick this in place with strong, clear glue. Let your puppet dry overnight, and it will be ready to make its debut!

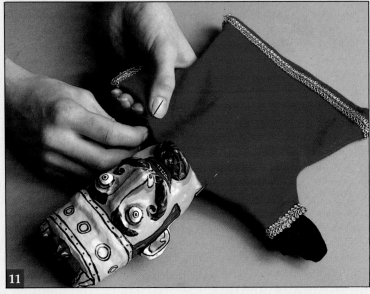